Vegan Junk Food

200+ VEGAN RECIPES FOR THE FOODS YOU CRAVE—
Minus the Ingredients You Don't

LANE GOLD

ADAMS MEDIA

NEW YORK   LONDON   TORONTO   SYDNEY   NEW DELHI

Adams Media
An Imprint of Simon & Schuster, Inc.
57 Littlefield Street
Avon, Massachusetts 02322

This Adams Media trade paperback edition October 2018

ADAMS MEDIA and colophon are trademarks of Simon & Schuster.

For information about special discounts for bulk purchases, please contact Simon & Schuster Special Sales at 1-866-506-1949 or business@simonandschuster.com.

The Simon & Schuster Speakers Bureau can bring authors to your live event. For more information or to book an event contact the Simon & Schuster Speakers Bureau at 1-866-248-3049 or visit our website at www.simonspeakers.com.

Interior design by Sylvia McArdle
Photographs by James Stefiuk

Manufactured in the United States of America

10 9 8 7 6 5 4 3 2

Library of Congress Cataloging-in-Publication Data
Gold, Lane, author.
Vegan junk food, expanded edition / Lane Gold.
Avon, Massachusetts: Adams Media, 2018.
Includes index.
LCCN 2018020540 | ISBN 9781507209035 (pb) | ISBN 9781507209042 (ebook)
Subjects: LCSH: Vegan cooking. | Junk food. | Vegetarian convenience foods. | LCGFT: Cookbooks.
Classification: LCC TX837 .G598 2018 | DDC 641.5/636--dc23
LC record available at https://lccn.loc.gov/2018020540

ISBN 978-1-5072-0903-5
ISBN 978-1-5072-0904-2 (ebook)

Contents

• CHAPTER 6 •

Dips for All Seasons 139

• CHAPTER 7 •

Savory Treats 160

• CHAPTER 8 •

Cakewalk (Pies, Too) 172

Introduction

There's a misconception that vegans want to eat only healthy foods. Wrong!
Vegans like deep-fried foods, sugary foods, and fatty foods just like everyone
else. Just because food is animal friendly doesn't mean it can't also be indul-
gent and delicious. And while in the past it was difficult for vegans to find the
foods they craved, there are now entire sections of grocery stores loaded with
vegan products. From chocolate chips, mayonnaise, cheese, sour cream, and
ice cream, to sliced deli meats, boxed mac and cheese, and frozen pizza—it
seems there isn't a single corner of the retail market untouched by vegan
ingenuity.

The more than 200 recipes within these pages span the savory to the sweet,
but they all reflect the fact that vegans want to eat junk food too (and by "junk"
I mean delicious!). Whether you are looking for something to make for dinner,
a dish to take to a party, or a deliciously sinful indulgence that doesn't harm
animals—this book has all your bases covered. From the perfect Mac and
Cheese Bake, and a Black Bean Burger with Onion Rings, to the Caesar Salad
Dressing you crave, and a delicious Rich Chocolate Cake with Chocolate
Ganache no one can believe is vegan, *Vegan Junk Food, Expanded Edition* has a
dish for any occasion.

At a time when it's easier than ever to find vegan products or restaurants,
there's still something deeply satisfying about making a homemade meal in
your own kitchen. Some of the recipes in this book are quick and easy, using
readily found grocery store items, and others require more time and patience or
perhaps a small journey to find select ingredients. Whichever you choose, I have
tried to simplify the recipes and make even basic things like yeasted breads,
pizza dough, and layered cakes filled with flavor.

Food is joy, and vegans want to experience that pleasure too. With *Vegan
Junk Food, Expanded Edition*, you'll be able to make the foods you crave in a
delicious and animal-friendly way. No longer will you have to stare longingly
through bakery shop windows or be stuck eating carrot sticks at parties—
now you'll be able to get your junk food cravings satisfied. So if you're ready
to indulge in the deliciously junky side of vegan cooking, let's get started!

Vegan Essentials

In order to veganize nonvegan goodies, you need to become familiar with a whole host of ingredients that'll become your best allies in the kitchen. Here's a guide to the animal-friendly pantry items that help make your junk food taste oh-so-good.

NONDAIRY MILK

For recipes in this book that specify using nondairy milk, any of the following unsweetened milks will work: almond milk, hemp milk, rice milk, coconut milk, or soy milk. Choose the one you prefer to drink. When soy milk is specifically listed as an ingredient, it is usually for the body that it lends to the finished product. Other nondairy milks might not work well in that particular recipe; for example, rice milk tends to be a little more watery and may change the finished product's consistency. Replace soy milk in a recipe with a milk equal in body, such as hemp, coconut, or almond milk.

VEGAN BUTTER

Look for brands of vegan butter that are non-hydrogenated and are trans-fat-free. When baking, opt for vegan butter sticks, as they tend to have less water content and are easier to measure. One great brand to try is Earth Balance (www.earthbalancenatural.com).

NONHYDROGENATED VEGAN SHORTENING

While it does not impart any flavor, shortening is great for making pie crusts because it is better able to coat flour than butter—a key to flaky pastry. For frosting it is also great, as it doesn't melt at room temperature. Try Spectrum brand shortening (www.spectrumorganics.com).

VEGETABLE OIL

Here's the rundown on the different oils I recommend for your junk food recipes. The term *oil* used in recipes can apply to any of the oils discussed in this section.

- **Extra-virgin olive oil**—This is best for sautéing savory items, and it can also be used for baking where oil is called for, but it can impart a strong flavor.
- **Canola oil or soybean oil**—Their neutral flavor is ideal for baking.
- **Virgin coconut oil**—This works best in desserts, as it has a light coconut flavor and pairs well with chocolate. As with all oils, look for organic varieties. Nutiva is a good brand to try (www.nutiva.com).

SUGAR

Table sugar, powdered sugar, or most brown sugar is not vegan because of the use of animal bone char to filter it. Most brown sugar starts as white sugar that has molasses added to it later, and powdered sugar starts as table sugar that is then ground into a powder with cornstarch. Alternatives to these sugars are many and include unrefined cane sugar, evaporated cane juice, beet sugar, date sugar, raw or turbinado sugar, and coconut sugar. The term *sugar* used in recipes can apply to any of the sugars or sweeteners discussed in this section. Here are some one-to-one replacements:

- **Table sugar**—Use vegan cane sugar, beet sugar, or granulated and dehydrated cane juice. Florida Crystals offers a vegan version: www.floridacrystals.com.

- **Brown sugar**—Use Sucanat, a whole-cane sugar.

- **Powdered sugar**—Use powdered sugar that is made from organic sugar cane.

- **Liquid sugars**—Use in recipes where you don't mind the additional flavor and softened texture that liquid sugars lend to baked goods. Agave, barley malt syrup, brown rice syrup, molasses, corn syrup (not to fear: although this is a sugar, it's not the same as high-fructose corn syrup), and pure maple syrup are good for baking and candy making. Raw agave syrup is a good replacement for honey.

MEAT ALTERNATIVES

Fake meat is a big part of vegan junk food, so here's a rundown.

- **Seitan, or wheat meat**—Made from vital wheat gluten and flavorings, seitan has a chewy texture and can be flavored with seasonings to imitate many meat forms. Packaged in broth, prepared seitan is great for stir-fries and many other dishes that call for slabs of meat.

- **Frozen meat crumbles and patties**—The freezer section of your favorite organic grocery should be well stocked with all sorts of brands.

- **Hot dogs**—Try Yves Veggie Cuisine (www.yvesveggie.com). For beer brats, try Tofurky brand (www.tofurky.com).

- **Soy chorizo**—Made from textured vegetable protein (TVP for short) and spices, this is a vegan version of a Mexican sausage made with marinated and minced meat that's perfect with tofu scramble and tucked into tortillas. Look for "Soyrizo," as it's commonly marketed that way.

EGG REPLACERS

In baking, flaxseeds do a nice job of replacing eggs. Ground into a powder and then mixed with water, flaxseeds create a gelatinous mixture that replaces the water weight, texture, and some of the fat in eggs, giving you fluffy cakes and cookies. Applesauce is another egg stand-in for baking, but can impart an apple flavor and a lot of sweetness (be sure to reduce the sugar in recipes if you are using applesauce in place of eggs). Blended tofu is a great binder in vegan quiches and crepes where an egg would add denseness and form. And a teaspoon of nutritional yeast or black salt is great at imparting egg flavor to tofu scrambles or vegan egg salad.

CHOCOLATE

Use varieties of chocolate that do not contain milk or lecithin, an emulsifier that can be made from animals (soy lecithin is vegan).

- **Chocolate chips**—Look for brands that don't contain milk, like Enjoy Life Food's (www.enjoylifefoods.com) morsels.

- **Chocolate bars**—For specialty candy bars, OCHO (www.ochocandy.com), Go Max Go Foods (http://gomaxgofoods.com), and Justin's (www.justins.com) offer a wide variety of tasty veganized standard candy products.

- **Cocoa powder**—Cocoa powder is made from cocoa beans and is vegan.

- **White bars**—Organic Nectars (www .organicnectars.com) offers raw organic white chocolate bars.
- **White chips**—Oppenheimer white chocolate chips melt nicely and hold up in a cookie. You can find them online at Food Fight! Grocery (www.foodfightgrocery.com).

MARSHMALLOWS

Seek out varieties of marshmallows that do not contain gelatin, which is an animal product.

Look for Dandies (www.chicagoveganfoods .com) and Trader Joe's (www.traderjoes.com) store brand.

SEASONINGS

Butler Chik-Style Seasoning (www.butlerfoods .com), Bragg Liquid Aminos (www.bragg.com), and kelp can help make things tasty and/or salty.

CHEESE

Cheese is an absolute must for pizza or for making your savory junk food, and there are lots of varieties of cheese shreds on the market. Follow Your Heart varieties are among the best (www.followyourheart.com). You can also try nutritional yeast to impart a cheesy flavor to many of your dishes.

CHAPTER 1

Breakfast of Champions

Something Savory, Lots of Sweets

SCRAMBLED TOFU BISCUIT SANDWICH
with SAUSAGE GRAVY

1 (16-ounce) package firm tofu, drained and broken up into small chunks

1 teaspoon oil

1 tablespoon nutritional yeast

½ teaspoon onion powder

⅛ teaspoon turmeric

2 teaspoons soy sauce

1 (14-ounce) package Lightlife Gimme Lean Sausage

1 tablespoon oil

¼ cup flour

2 cups nondairy milk

1 teaspoon salt

1 teaspoon black pepper

4 Drop Biscuits (see Chapter 4), baked, or 4 English muffins, toasted

Pair seasoned scrambled tofu with a savory sauce on a warm toasted biscuit for a sandwich that puts diner fare to shame. Just because it's vegan sausage doesn't mean it lacks the salty, rich flavor of the original. And the creaminess of the gravy can be achieved with nary a cow product in sight.

« – »

1. In a medium sauté pan over medium-high heat, cook tofu in oil 5 minutes.

2. Stir in nutritional yeast, onion powder, turmeric, and soy sauce, and cook 2 more minutes. Remove from pan.

3. Make the gravy: In the same pan, cook sausage in oil until browned. Stir in flour and cook 1 minute. Whisk in milk. Cook, stirring constantly, until thick and bubbly, about 4 minutes. Season with salt and pepper.

4. On a biscuit bottom half, spoon ¼ of scrambled tofu, smother it in gravy, cover with the biscuit top, and go to town.

RED BELL PEPPER, CARAMELIZED ONION, and HASH BROWN QUICHE

This eggless quiche gets its sweetness from the red bell peppers and onions and is ideal if you're looking for a savory way to start the day. Of course, you could make the crust by slicing and parboiling potatoes, but why bother? Junk food by definition should be easy, and packaged hash browns crisp up just right.

» SERVES 6 «

1 medium onion, peeled and chopped

1 medium red bell pepper, seeded and sliced

½ teaspoon salt

3 teaspoons oil

1 (30-ounce) package hash browns

1 (16-ounce) package firm tofu, drained

¼ cup Vegan Sour Cream (see Chapter 6)

3 tablespoons nutritional yeast

½ teaspoon garlic powder

1 teaspoon salt

½ teaspoon black pepper

¼ teaspoon red pepper flakes

1. Preheat oven to 350°F. Lightly grease a 9" × 13" baking dish or 2 (8") round baking pans.

2. In a medium sauté pan over medium-high heat, sauté onions, bell peppers, and salt in oil until onion begins to turn deep golden brown, about 12 minutes. Remove from heat.

3. Press hash browns into prepared baking dish. Cover with onions and bell peppers.

4. Crumble tofu into a food processor with Vegan Sour Cream, nutritional yeast, garlic powder, salt, and pepper until very smooth.

5. Pour over onions and bell peppers, sprinkle with red pepper flakes.

6. Bake 45–50 minutes, checking periodically to make sure it doesn't brown too soon. If that happens, cover with foil.

7. Allow to cool slightly and dig in.

POTATO SOYRIZO OMELET

½ cup firm tofu

1½ cups nondairy milk

2 teaspoons oil

1 cup flour

2 tablespoons nutritional yeast

1½ teaspoons baking powder

1 teaspoon salt

⅛ teaspoon turmeric

1 tablespoon chopped chives

2 tablespoons oil, divided

4 medium potatoes, peeled and diced

6 ounces Soyrizo vegan Mexican sausage

½ teaspoon salt

½ teaspoon black pepper

Nutritional yeast is a vegan's best friend. Add it to tofu and the result is a flavor reminiscent of eggs. Here you get an omelet that's more like a delicate crepe, with a bold flavored topping that's anything but delicate.

« – »

1. In a blender, blend tofu, milk, and 2 teaspoons oil until smooth.

2. In a medium bowl, combine flour, nutritional yeast, baking powder, salt, turmeric, and chives. Add blended ingredients to flour mixture and mix until very smooth.

3. In a 12" skillet over medium-high heat, cook ⅓ cup batter at a time in about 1 teaspoon oil. Swirl batter in the pan so that it fills the entire bottom of the pan. Flip pancake over when the edges look dry and the bottom is golden brown; cook the second side until golden brown as well. Keep pancakes warm covered in foil in the oven at low heat.

4. To make potato-Soyrizo filling, heat remaining oil in a large nonstick pan over medium-high heat, add potatoes, and cover with a tight-fitting lid.

5. Cook potatoes, turning as the bottom ones become golden, removing lid after 15 minutes, and cooking an additional 5–10 minutes.

6. When potatoes are golden and cooked through, add Soyrizo, salt, and pepper to the pan and cook just long enough to heat through, about 2 minutes.

7. To assemble omelet, place a pancake on a plate, place about ¾ cup of potato mixture on one half, and fold over.

CHOCOLATE *and* HAZELNUT SCONES

These scones are perfect anytime with a cup of tea or, even better, as a way to eat dessert for breakfast. They are great warm out of the oven, but don't be afraid to make them the day before.

« – »

1. Preheat oven to 450°F.

2. In a large bowl, stir together flour, sugar, baking powder, and salt.

3. Using a pastry cutter, incorporate butter into flour until you have coarse crumbs.

4. Add yogurt, chocolate chips, and hazelnuts and stir until everything is just moistened and mostly holding together. Turn out onto a parchment paper–lined baking sheet and form into an even 7" round. Cut the round into 8 wedges.

5. Bake 13–15 minutes, allow to cool briefly on baking sheet.

» SERVES 8 «

2¼ cups flour

⅓ cup sugar

1 tablespoon baking powder

½ teaspoon salt

½ cup cold vegan butter

1 cup unsweetened coconut milk yogurt

½ cup vegan chocolate chips

½ cup chopped toasted hazelnuts

CINNAMON ROLLS

My 15-year-old has laid claim to making these heaven-ly scented rounds of sweetness for a few years now, so don't worry about the many steps or trying your hand at proofing yeast—it's a snap. This recipe also doubles easily.

«------------------------------»

1. Combine milk, yeast, and ¼ teaspoon sugar in a small bowl, allow to proof 15 minutes. Add remaining sugar, butter, flax-seed mixture, and vanilla. Mix to combine.

2. Add flour, salt, and nutmeg to an electric mixing bowl fitted with a dough blade. While on low setting, add yeast mixture to flour. Mix 5 minutes. Cover and let rise in a warm place 1 hour.

3. Preheat oven to 350°F.

4. Roll dough out into a rectangle ½" thick.

5. Combine filling ingredients in a medium bowl and spread filling mixture out on the dough, leaving a few inches of dough clean at a long edge. Roll one long edge tightly toward the clean edge, press to seal.

6. Using a sharp serrated knife cut the roll into 1½" slices. Place slices flat side down onto a greased 9" × 13" baking dish.

7. Bake 35 minutes or until top is golden.

8. While the rolls are baking, combine frosting ingredients in a medium bowl. Pour over rolls hot from the oven. Serve immediately.

» SERVES 8 «

1 cup nondairy milk, heated to 100°F

2½ teaspoons instant yeast

¼ cup sugar, divided

4 tablespoons vegan butter

1 tablespoon ground flaxseeds plus 4 tablespoons water, combined

1½ teaspoons vanilla extract

2¾ cups flour

¾ teaspoon salt

½ teaspoon ground nutmeg

FILLING

¼ cup vegan butter, room temperature

½ cup sugar

3 tablespoons ground cinnamon

FROSTING

2 cups powdered sugar

⅓ cup nondairy milk

4 tablespoons vegan butter

1 teaspoon vanilla extract

SWEET POTATO HASH
with GREEN CHILIES

» SERVES 4 «

- 4 medium sweet potatoes, peeled and chopped
- 1 medium green chili such as poblano or Hatch
- 1 small onion, peeled and chopped
- 2 tablespoons coconut oil
- 1 teaspoon salt

Earthy sweet potatoes and roasted chilies are a perfect match for a late breakfast after a late night out.

« – – – – – – – – – – – – – – – – – – – »

1. Drop sweet potatoes into a large pot of boiling water and cook until just tender through the middle, about 10 minutes.

2. While potatoes are cooking, place chili directly on the burner of your stove, turning to char evenly; alternatively, you can use a cast-iron pan or the broiler portion of your oven to get a black char on the skin. Place chili in a paper bag for 5 minutes to steam, making the skins easier to release. Remove skin, and deseed and chop chili.

3. Drain potatoes well. Add onions to a medium heavy-bottomed fry pan with coconut oil over medium heat. Cook until translucent, about 5 minutes. Add potatoes, chilies, and salt.

4. Cook until onions are caramelized and potatoes are starting to slightly crisp, about 5 minutes.

5. Serve immediately.

EGGPLANT BACON

This is so delicious; I've known people (not naming names) who devour a plate in one sitting. Better be preemptive and make two batches! Liquid smoke is the key ingredient here, giving you a smoky bacon flavor without animal by-products.

» SERVES 6 «

2 medium eggplants
½ cup light soy sauce
¼ cup brown sugar
¼ cup apple cider vinegar
¼ cup olive oil
½ teaspoon black pepper
⅛ teaspoon liquid smoke
1 teaspoon Cajun-style seasoned salt (optional)

1. Remove stem end of eggplants, stand eggplants on cut end, and slice down in very thin strips about ⅛" thick. A mandoline works great for this.

2. In a large bowl, whisk together soy sauce, brown sugar, vinegar, oil, pepper, liquid smoke, and seasoned salt if using.

3. Place eggplant strips in marinade, making sure that each strip gets coated. Allow to marinate in the refrigerator 3–4 hours, occasionally turning eggplant to be sure all strips are getting evenly marinated.

4. Preheat oven to 350°F. Line a cookie sheet with parchment paper, lightly greased.

5. Place eggplant strips on prepared cookie sheet. Do not overlap, but close together is fine.

6. Bake about 20 minutes; do not overbake. Eggplant strips will crisp as they cool.

7. Alternatively, the strips can be made in a food dehydrator on medium heat for 24 hours or when they reach the desired crispness.

PERFECT HASH BROWNS

2 pounds potatoes, peeled and quartered

2 teaspoons salt, divided

¼ cup grated onion

½ teaspoon black pepper

2 tablespoons vegan butter

2 tablespoons oil

Making homemade diner-style hash browns will make you seem like a rock star to those lucky enough to get a bite. They're crispy, salty, and easy to prepare. Make your morning even easier by boiling the potatoes the night before.

1. Place potatoes in a 4-quart saucepan over high heat and pour in enough water to cover potatoes; add 1 teaspoon salt.

2. When potatoes come to a boil, allow them to cook 5 minutes, then remove from heat.

3. Grate potatoes into a medium bowl using a box grater. Gently stir in grated onion and sprinkle on remaining salt and pepper; mix gently.

4. In a large sauté pan over medium-high heat, heat 1 tablespoon butter with 1 tablespoon oil. When butter is sizzling, add a heaping tablespoonful of potatoes and flatten slightly with a spatula.

5. Fry two or three tablespoonfuls at a time, depending on the size of pan. Cook 5 minutes or until crispy and golden brown, flip over with a spatula, and cook the other side until crispy. Add more oil and butter to the pan before cooking the next batch.

TATER TOTS BREAKFAST CASSEROLE

Sometimes I think the fact that Tater Tots exist—and are vegan—proves there is a god. But honestly, when you combine them with the sausage-tofu mixture to make this savory casserole, it borders on divine. This is also a great option for brunch: prep the night before and bake in the morning. Easy and tasty!

1 (14-ounce) package Lightlife Gimme Lean Sausage

1 tablespoon oil

1 (16-ounce) package firm tofu, drained

½ cup nutritional yeast

2 teaspoons finely chopped chives

2 teaspoons salt

½ teaspoon black pepper

½ teaspoon garlic powder

1 (16-ounce) package frozen Tater Tots

1. Preheat oven to 350°F. Lightly oil a 9" × 13" baking dish.

2. In a medium sauté pan over medium-high heat, cook sausage in oil, breaking it up into bite-sized pieces. Cook until browned.

3. In a blender, process tofu until very smooth. Add nutritional yeast, chives, salt, pepper, and garlic powder, blending until incorporated.

4. Pour blended mixture into prepared baking dish. Add sausage and mix just to distribute sausage evenly.

5. Arrange Tater Tots on top of tofu mixture.

6. Bake 45–50 minutes or until potatoes are lightly browned. Tofu will continue to firm as it cools, about 30 minutes.

SAUSAGE in a BLANKET with GLAZED APPLES

1 (8-ounce) package Tofurky Breakfast Links (vegan)

¼ cup water

½ cup brown sugar

2 medium Granny Smith apples, peeled, cored, and chopped

1 cup flour

¼ cup quick-cooking oats

2 teaspoons baking powder

½ teaspoon salt

1½ cups nondairy milk

2 tablespoons sugar

1 tablespoon oil

1 recipe Vegan Sour Cream (see Chapter 6) (optional)

Salty-sweet goodness! This recipe combines the best of breakfast foods—the meaty flavor of sausage, the fluffy carb-load of pancakes, and the caramel sweetness of homemade applesauce—all rolled into one delicious dish.

1. In a medium nonstick pan over medium-high heat, cook breakfast links until they are heated through and browned. Set aside.

2. In a medium saucepan over medium-high heat, bring water and brown sugar to a boil; continue to cook 1 minute, add apples, and cook until sauce has thickened and apples are tender, about 10 minutes.

3. In a medium bowl, combine flour, oats, baking powder, and salt. Gently stir in milk, sugar, and oil just until combined; a few lumps are okay.

4. Cook each ⅓ cup of pancake batter on a lightly oiled nonstick pan over medium-high heat, flipping when bubbles appear on the surface of the pancake; cook the second side until golden.

5. To assemble, roll a Breakfast Link inside each pancake and top with caramelized apples. If you like, add a dollop of Vegan Sour Cream.

BRUNCH BENEDICT

Veganizing this classic brunch dish merely involves perfecting the hollandaise. Cashews provide richness and creaminess, while the lemon and nutritional yeast lend the tang. Problem solved.

» SERVES 4 «

1 cup cashews

1 cup silken tofu, drained

1 tablespoon oil

¼ cup lemon juice

1 tablespoon nutritional yeast

½ teaspoon salt

½ teaspoon black pepper

⅛ teaspoon turmeric

1 tablespoon chopped fresh chives

4 medium plain bagels

2 tablespoons vegan butter

1 (5.5-ounce) package vegan deli slices, such as Tofurky Deli Slices Hickory Smoked

1. In a food processor with a fitted blade, process cashews until very fine.

2. Add tofu, oil, lemon juice, nutritional yeast, salt, pepper, and turmeric, and process until very smooth, about 4 minutes.

3. In a medium saucepan over low heat, warm cashew sauce, being very careful not to boil. Remove from heat and stir in chives.

4. While the sauce is heating, toast bagels and spread on butter. Top each bagel half with four deli slices. Serve topped with warmed cashew hollandaise.

PECAN PIE MUFFINS

Who says you can't have pie for breakfast? This just makes it easier because the muffins are quick to prepare, and you portion them out into paper-lined tins for individual servings. They're so buttery and nutty, it's unlikely they'll be around for long...

» MAKES 12 MUFFINS «

½ cup nondairy milk

2 tablespoons ground flaxseeds

1 cup crushed pecans

1 cup packed brown sugar

½ cup flour

½ cup vegan butter, melted

1. Preheat oven to 350°F.

2. Combine milk with flaxseeds in a small bowl and set aside.

3. In a large mixing bowl, combine pecans, brown sugar, and flour. Add in flaxseed mixture along with the butter and mix just until combined.

4. Pour into 12 paper-lined muffin tins; fill about ¾ full.

5. Bake 25 minutes, serve warm.

BLUEBERRY STREUSEL MUFFINS

» MAKES 12 MUFFINS «

1 tablespoon ground flaxseeds

1½ cups soy milk

1 tablespoon apple cider vinegar

½ cup nonhydrogenated vegetable shortening

2 tablespoons vegan butter

1¼ cups sugar

1 teaspoon vanilla extract

3 cups flour

2½ teaspoons baking powder

½ teaspoon salt

1½ cups fresh blueberries

STREUSEL TOPPING

½ cup vegan butter, softened

¼ cup brown sugar

¼ cup sugar

⅔ cup flour

¼ teaspoon ground cinnamon

⅛ teaspoon salt

Sugar, butter, shortening, salt, more sugar...this is a textbook junk food breakfast, which means it's mouth-watering good. It's also loaded with streusel topping and blueberries. (At least the blueberries have some redeeming qualities.)

1. Preheat oven to 375°F. Line a 12-cup muffin tin with 12 paper liners.

2. In a small bowl, mix flaxseeds, soy milk, and vinegar; set aside.

3. In a stand mixer or by hand, beat shortening, butter, sugar, and vanilla until light and fluffy.

4. In a medium bowl, sift flour, baking powder, and salt.

5. Add milk mixture to shortening and beat until combined. Stir in flour mixture and mix just until combined; fold in blueberries; do not overmix.

6. Fill prepared muffin tins ¾ full.

7. Make the topping: in a medium bowl, combine butter, brown sugar, sugar, flour, cinnamon, and salt with a fork until butter is well mixed in and crumbly. Spoon by the heaping tablespoonful onto muffins.

8. Bake 30 minutes. Cool slightly and slather with extra vegan butter so that it melts onto the muffin.

BANANA CHOCOLATE CHIP MUFFINS

Perfect for when you really want cake for breakfast, these moist muffins emit the most sinful banana-vanilla aroma while they're cooking. The chocolate chips and toasty oatmeal crumble are just icing on the cake—er, muffin.

« – »

1. Preheat oven to 375°F. Line a 12-cup muffin tin with 12 paper liners.

2. In a large bowl, combine flaxseeds, soy milk, and vinegar; set aside.

3. In a medium bowl, sift flour, baking powder, baking soda, and salt.

4. Add banana, oil, and vanilla to milk mixture, stirring to combine.

5. Stir in flour mixture and mix gently to combine; do not overmix. Fold in chocolate chips.

6. Fill prepared muffin tins ¾ full.

7. In a small bowl, combine oats, sugar, butter, and salt until crumbly.

8. Spoon on top of muffin batter by the heaping tablespoonful. Press lightly to make sure it doesn't crumble off as the muffin puffs.

9. Bake 30 minutes or until golden brown.

» MAKES 12 MUFFINS «

2 tablespoons ground flaxseeds

¾ cup soy milk

1 tablespoon apple cider vinegar

3 cups flour

2 teaspoons baking powder

1 teaspoon baking soda

1 teaspoon salt

1½ cups mashed banana

1 cup vegetable oil

1½ teaspoons vanilla extract

1 cup vegan chocolate chips

STREUSEL TOPPING

1 cup quick-cooking oats

½ cup sugar

5 tablespoons vegan butter, softened

½ teaspoon salt

CHEESECAKE-FILLED CRUMB CAKE

¾ cup soy milk

1 tablespoon apple cider vinegar

2 cups flour

½ teaspoon baking soda

2 teaspoons baking powder

½ teaspoon salt

½ teaspoon ground cinnamon

½ cup oil

1 cup sugar

FILLING

1 (8-ounce) container vegan cream cheese, softened

⅓ cup sugar

2 tablespoons flour

2 teaspoons lemon zest

½ teaspoon salt

½ teaspoon vanilla extract

TOPPING

⅔ cup packed brown sugar

½ cup flour

1 teaspoon ground cinnamon

¼ teaspoon ground nutmeg

½ teaspoon salt

⅔ cup vegan butter, softened

Here's another example of a breakfast "dessert" on steroids. For days when crumb cake à la Hostess just won't cut it, go the extra mile and create this creamy sensation.

« – »

1. Preheat oven to 350°F. Lightly grease a 9" × 9" baking dish.

2. Combine soy milk and vinegar in a medium bowl; set aside 5 minutes to thicken.

3. In a large mixing bowl, add flour, baking soda, baking powder, salt, and cinnamon.

4. Add oil and sugar to soy milk mixture, stirring to combine.

5. Add wet ingredients to dry ingredients and stir until mixture is completely smooth. Pour half of batter into prepared baking dish.

6. Make the filling: In a medium bowl, mix cream cheese and sugar together. Add flour, lemon zest, salt, and vanilla extract. Pour over batter layer. Cover with remaining batter.

7. Make the topping: in a small bowl, mix together brown sugar, flour, cinnamon, nutmeg, salt, and butter. Crumble over cake.

8. Bake 35–40 minutes or until topping is golden brown. Let cool completely before cutting.

APPLE FRITTERS

When you wake up with a hankering for something warm, sweet, and tart, pad to the kitchen in your jammies and slippers and whip up a batch of these golden-fried apple fritters. Your pastries will be ready to eat before your coffee's done brewing. (Mission to remain in PJs: accomplished.)

1 cup cake flour*

1 tablespoon sugar

1 teaspoon baking powder

¼ teaspoon salt

1 tablespoon ground flaxseeds

½ cup nondairy milk

1½ tablespoons vegan butter, melted

½ teaspoon vanilla extract

1 cup peeled and chopped tart baking apples (Granny Smith or Honeycrisp)

Oil (for frying)

Powdered sugar (for dusting)

*NOTE: If you do not have cake flour, measure 2 tablespoons cornstarch into a 1-cup dry measuring cup and add all-purpose flour until it is full, leveling off flour with the back of a knife. Sift together.

1. Combine flour, sugar, baking powder, and salt in a large bowl.

2. In a medium bowl, combine flaxseeds, milk, butter, and vanilla. Add wet ingredients to dry mixture and stir until just combined. Gently stir in apples. Do not overmix.

3. In a large, deep sauté pan over medium-high heat, bring about 1" oil to 360°F.

4. Carefully drop batter by heaping tablespoonful into oil, frying until golden brown on each side, about 4–5 minutes.

5. Drain on a paper towel. Sprinkle with powdered sugar.

BAKED DONUT HOLES 3-WAYS

» MAKES 24
DONUT HOLES «

1½ cups flour

⅓ cup oil

½ cup sugar

½ cup nondairy milk

1 tablespoon ground flaxseeds

1½ teaspoons baking powder

½ teaspoon salt

¼ teaspoon ground nutmeg

As far as I know, there are only a handful of bakeries that specialize in vegan donuts—and many don't ship 'em. If you're lucky enough to live in a part of the world that has these magical bakeries, by all means seek them out. For everyone else, here's an easy way to make your own.

« – »

1. Preheat oven to 350°F.

2. Combine all ingredients in a medium bowl until smooth.

3. Lightly grease a mini-muffin tin. Fill each halfway with batter.

4. Bake 15 minutes or until a toothpick comes out clean.

Cinnamon Sugar Donuts

Roll each donut in a mixture of ½ cup sugar mixed with 1 teaspoon cinnamon while still warm.

Powdered Donuts

Roll each donut in 1 cup powdered sugar while still hot, allow to cool, and roll again.

Chocolate Glaze Donuts

Remove donuts from pan and allow to cool. In a small microwave-safe bowl, heat 1 (12-ounce) package vegan chocolate chips with 1 tablespoon coconut oil in increments of 15 seconds, stirring after each until melted. Using two forks, dip each donut, turning to coat evenly and allowing extra chocolate to drip off. Place on a sheet of parchment paper and refrigerate until chocolate is firm. Alternatively, while chocolate is still wet, sprinkle each donut with chopped nuts, coconut, or sprinkles.

OATMEAL BRÛLÉE *with* VANILLA CREAM SAUCE

» SERVES 4 «

1 cup old-fashioned oats

1½ cups soy creamer or nondairy milk

3 tablespoons brown sugar

1 tablespoon vegan butter

½ teaspoon salt

½ cup fresh raspberries or blackberries

¼ cup sugar

Did someone say brûlée? For breakfast? You betcha. This super-creamy oatmeal has a sugar crust and a fresh berry surprise at the bottom. With a drizzle of the Vanilla Cream Sauce, you've got the makings of gourmet junk food.

1. Preheat oven to broil setting. Lightly grease four large or six small ovenproof ramekins.

2. In a medium saucepan over medium heat, combine oats, soy creamer or nondairy milk, brown sugar, butter, and salt. Cook 3–5 minutes.

3. Place berries in prepared ramekins, then top with cooked oatmeal. Sprinkle sugar over each, covering the surface completely.

4. Place ramekins under broiler for about 2 minutes. Watch carefully, because once the sugar melts, it will go quickly from golden to burnt.

5. Serve brûlée hot with Vanilla Cream Sauce on the side.

Vanilla Cream Sauce

1 cup soy creamer*

1 teaspoon cornstarch

2 teaspoons vanilla extract

*NOTE: If you don't have soy creamer, you can use 1 cup nondairy milk plus 1 tablespoon cornstarch to achieve the same creamy results.

In a medium saucepan over medium-high heat, bring soy creamer and cornstarch to a boil, stirring constantly; continue to cook 1 minute. Remove from heat and stir in vanilla. (This sauce can be served hot or can be refrigerated and served cold.)

PUMPKIN PIE PANCAKES *with* CINNAMON SYRUP

These pancakes are easier than pie—with all the same flavors. Top with a buttery cinnamon syrup that'll make your omnivorous friends jealous.

1. In a medium bowl, combine milk, flaxseeds, pumpkin, and oil, and stir well.

2. In a large bowl, sift together flour, sugar, baking powder, pumpkin pie spice, and salt. Add wet ingredients to dry mixture, stirring gently until just combined. A few lumps are okay.

3. Cook ⅓ cup of pancake batter on a lightly oiled nonstick pan over medium-high heat, flipping when bubbles appear on the surface of the pancake; cook the second side until golden.

Cinnamon Syrup

1. In a small saucepan over medium-high heat, stir butter until bubbly and golden brown. Add brown sugar, stirring constantly, and cook until it comes back to a boil. Remove from heat and add vanilla and cinnamon.

2. Serve warm over piping-hot pancakes.

» SERVES 4 «

1 cup nondairy milk

2 tablespoons ground flaxseeds

½ cup canned pure pumpkin

2 tablespoons oil

1¼ cups flour

1 tablespoon sugar

2 teaspoons baking powder

1 teaspoon pumpkin pie spice

½ teaspoon salt

½ cup vegan butter

½ cup brown sugar

1 teaspoon vanilla extract

2 teaspoons ground cinnamon

PEANUT BUTTER PANCAKES *with* STRAWBERRY JAM

1 cup nondairy milk

2 tablespoons ground flaxseeds

1½ cups flour

1 tablespoon sugar

2 teaspoons baking powder

½ teaspoon salt

½ cup peanut butter

½ teaspoon vanilla extract

Strawberry jam

A new twist on a classic lunch treat, this breakfast PB&J satisfies the urge to be back in middle school with your homies. (Don't be fooled by the flaxseeds! I'm not trying to make this healthy—mixed with milk, they're a great substitute binder in place of eggs.)

1. In a small bowl, mix milk and flaxseeds, then set aside.

2. In a medium bowl, whisk together flour, sugar, baking powder, and salt.

3. Mix peanut butter and vanilla into milk mixture. Stir well. Add to flour mixture and stir just until combined. Do not overmix; a few lumps are okay.

4. Cook each ⅓ cup of pancake batter on a lightly oiled nonstick pan over medium-high heat, flipping when bubbles appear on the surface of the pancake and then cooking the second side until golden.

5. Serve with a dollop of your favorite strawberry jam.

CINNAMON ROLL FRENCH TOAST

Here's the perfect solution for your leftover French bread, and one that rivals the gooiest, sweet, decadent cinnamon rolls found in a tube in the refrigerator aisle. Pair this dish with Eggplant Bacon (see recipe in this chapter) and fresh-squeezed OJ for a brunch extravaganza.

1. In a shallow dish, whisk together milk, flour, nutritional yeast, cinnamon, sugar, and salt.

2. To make the glaze, in a small bowl, mix together melted butter, cinnamon, and sugar until sugar melts. Set aside.

3. Dip bread into milk mixture and fry in a medium sauté pan over medium heat with 1 teaspoon oil until browned on each side. Remove from pan and spread with a teaspoon of cinnamon glaze mixture. Repeat for the rest of bread slices.

4. To make the icing, in a small bowl, combine powdered sugar, butter, vanilla, and milk with a whisk until smooth. Drizzle over hot French toast and serve.

» SERVES 4 «

1½ cups nondairy milk

1½ tablespoons flour

2 tablespoons nutritional yeast

2 teaspoons ground cinnamon

1 tablespoon sugar

½ teaspoon salt

6 slices day-old thick-sliced French bread

Oil (for frying)

CINNAMON GLAZE

3 tablespoons vegan butter, melted

1 teaspoon ground cinnamon

2 teaspoons sugar

ICING

1 cup powdered sugar

1 tablespoon vegan butter, softened

1 teaspoon vanilla extract

2 tablespoons nondairy milk

EGGNOG FRENCH TOAST *with* BUTTER RUM SAUCE

1½ cups nondairy soy eggnog

1½ tablespoons flour

2 tablespoons nutritional yeast

½ teaspoon ground cinnamon

¼ cup sugar

½ teaspoon salt

6 slices day-old thick-sliced bread

Oil (for frying)

1 cup sugar

½ cup vegan butter

½ cup soy creamer or nondairy milk

⅛ teaspoon rum extract, or 2 tablespoons rum

Here's a festive breakfast treat that's perfect to serve to your vegan and omnivore friends and relatives—they'll never know what hit them. The eggnog flavor screams "Holiday!" and the Butter Rum Sauce is all about celebrating.

1. In a shallow dish, whisk together eggnog, flour, nutritional yeast, cinnamon, sugar, and salt until combined.

2. Dip each piece of bread into eggnog mixture. Fry in a large sauté pan over medium-high heat with 1 teaspoon oil until browned on each side.

Butter Rum Sauce

1. In a small saucepan over medium heat, combine sugar, butter, and creamer or milk, stirring constantly. Bring to a boil and continue to cook 1 minute. Remove from heat.

2. Stir in rum extract or rum and serve over French toast.

WAFFLES *with* CREAMY MAPLE SAUCE

If you don't currently own a waffle iron, you might want to knock on your neighbor's door and borrow one ASAP, because it would be a shame if you couldn't make these crisp, nutty-flax waffles and top them with a creamy, sweet maple sauce reminiscent of a donut glaze. Uh, what are you waiting for?

« – »

1. In a small bowl, mix milk with flaxseeds and set aside.

2. In a large bowl, combine flour, baking powder, salt, and sugar.

3. Stir oil into milk mixture. Add wet ingredients to dry ingredients in the large bowl and mix thoroughly.

4. Cook according to the manufacturer's directions for your waffle maker.

Creamy Maple Sauce

In a small saucepan over medium heat, combine all ingredients, stirring until very smooth and bubbling about 5 minutes. If mixture becomes too thick, add more milk a tablespoon at a time. Serve immediately on waffles.

» SERVES 4 «

1 cup nondairy milk

1 tablespoon ground flaxseeds

1 cup flour

2 teaspoons baking powder

¼ teaspoon salt

1 tablespoon sugar

¼ cup oil

---

2 cups powdered sugar

1 tablespoon pure maple syrup

¼ cup soy creamer or nondairy milk

STICKY CARAMEL BAKED FRENCH TOAST

A bit more time intensive than some of the other breakfast recipes, but because the bread sits before it bakes, it soaks up the caramel, and the results are super sticky and rich.

« – »

1. In a small saucepan over medium heat, stir brown sugar, butter, and agave syrup until it comes to a boil. Continue to cook 1 minute and remove from heat.

2. Lightly grease a 9" × 13" baking dish and pour caramel mixture into prepared baking dish. Place bread over caramel.

3. In a small bowl, mix creamer or milk, flour, nutritional yeast, cinnamon, vanilla, sugar, and salt. Pour over bread. Let it sit at least 1 hour or overnight in the refrigerator.

4. When ready to cook, preheat oven to 350°F and bake 25–30 minutes, until golden brown.

5. Serve with more caramel sauce and a dusting of powdered sugar if you desire.

>> **SERVES 6** <<

1 cup packed brown sugar

½ cup vegan butter

2 tablespoons agave syrup

6 slices day-old thick-sliced bread cut in half to make triangles

1 cup soy creamer or nondairy milk

1½ tablespoons flour

2 tablespoons nutritional yeast

1 teaspoon ground cinnamon

1 teaspoon vanilla extract

¼ cup sugar

½ teaspoon salt

LEMON POPPY SEED WAFFLES
with LEMON CURD

» SERVES 4 «

¾ cup nondairy milk

¼ cup lemon juice

1 tablespoon ground flaxseeds

Zest of 1 medium lemon

1 tablespoon sugar

¼ cup oil

1 cup flour

2 teaspoons baking powder

2 teaspoons poppy seeds

¼ teaspoon salt

¼ cup coconut milk

½ cup sugar

3 tablespoons cornstarch

⅛ teaspoon salt

Zest of 2 medium lemons

¼ cup lemon juice

These could just as easily fit into the dessert chapter, but as the saying goes, life is short, so eat dessert first. In this case, the first meal is breakfast, so it all makes sense. Sweet and tart, the yummy Lemon Curd could be eaten on its own by the spoonful (not that I've ever done that or anything).

« – »

1. In a small bowl, mix milk, lemon juice, flaxseeds, lemon zest, sugar, and oil, then set aside.

2. In a large bowl, combine flour, baking powder, poppy seeds, and salt.

3. Stir milk mixture into flour mixture and mix thoroughly.

4. Cook according to the manufacturer's directions for your waffle maker.

Lemon Curd

1. Combine coconut milk, sugar, cornstarch, salt, and lemon zest in a small saucepan. Heat over medium heat, stirring constantly, until mixture comes to a full boil, then cook 1 minute.

2. Remove from heat and stir in lemon juice. Serve warm over waffles. Be sure to refrigerate any leftover curd. (That is, if you have any leftovers!)

STRAWBERRY DAIQUIRI CREPES

There's no need to make a brunch cocktail to go with this dish, because rum is already part of the sauce. But these crepes won't make you tipsy; the prevalent flavor is that of fresh and frozen strawberries alongside delicate crepe quarters.

« – »

1. In a large mixing bowl, whisk together flour, milk, club soda, butter, nutritional yeast, and salt until smooth. Allow mixture to stand on counter 10 minutes.

2. Heat a 10" crepe pan or a shallow skillet over medium-high heat. Add about 1 teaspoon oil and swirl to coat bottom of pan. Add ¼ cup crepe mixture to pan and swirl again to coat entire bottom of pan with batter. Flip when edges look dry and bottom is just golden.

3. Transfer to a plate, fold each crepe into quarters, and cover with a towel to keep warm.

4. When ready to serve, place folded crepes on a plate, serve with hot Daiquiri Sauce, and garnish with fresh strawberries and powdered sugar.

Daiquiri Sauce

In a small saucepan over medium heat, heat strawberries and powdered sugar. Cook until liquid is reduced by half, about 8 minutes. Remove from heat, then stir in lime juice and rum. Serve hot.

» SERVES 4 «

1 cup flour

½ cup nondairy milk

½ cup club soda

¼ cup vegan butter, melted

1 tablespoon nutritional yeast

¼ teaspoon salt

Oil (for pan)

Fresh strawberries, hulled and quartered (for garnish)

Powdered sugar (for garnish)

4 ounces frozen strawberries

½ cup powdered sugar

⅛ cup lime juice

¼ cup rum

CHAPTER 2

Lunchtime Favorites

• Sandwiches, Wraps, Burgers, and Sliders •

SESAME TEMPEH SANDWICH

What would you prefer: a typical drive-thru burger or tempeh stewed in an Asian-inspired marinade, then pan-fried and topped with a fresh slaw and hot sauce? No contest, right?

« - »

1. In a shallow dish, combine soy sauce, sesame seeds, vinegar, ginger, sesame oil, and garlic. Add tempeh slices, turning to coat pieces. Marinate 1 hour or as long as overnight in the refrigerator, turning occasionally. Remove from marinade and set aside.

2. In a medium sauté pan over medium-high heat, sauté tempeh in peanut oil until golden on each side, about 4 minutes.

3. In a medium bowl, toss cabbage and carrots with rice vinegar, mayonnaise, soy sauce, and sesame oil.

4. On each split sandwich bun, place a few heaping tablespoons of slaw. Divide tempeh between the four rolls and top with an optional drizzle of chili sauce and/or hoisin sauce.

» SERVES 4 «

- 4 tablespoons light soy sauce
- 1 tablespoon sesame seeds, toasted
- 2 tablespoons balsamic vinegar
- 2 teaspoons minced ginger
- 2 teaspoons sesame oil
- 1 clove garlic, crushed
- 1 (8-ounce) package tempeh, sliced into ¼" slices
- 2 tablespoons peanut oil or olive oil
- 1 cup very thinly sliced green cabbage
- ½ cup very thinly sliced red cabbage
- 1 medium carrot, cut into long, thin strands
- 2 tablespoons seasoned rice vinegar
- 2 tablespoons vegan mayonnaise
- 1 teaspoon light soy sauce
- ½ teaspoon sesame oil
- 4 split sandwich buns
- Hot chili sauce or sriracha (optional)
- Hoisin sauce (optional)

BEET BURGER with BASIL MAYONNAISE

4 medium beets, tops removed

½ cup chickpea flour

1 medium yellow bell pepper, seeded and minced

2 cloves garlic, chopped

½ medium red onion, peeled and minced

1 teaspoon salt

½ teaspoon black pepper

2 tablespoons olive oil

6 whole-wheat hamburger buns, toasted

BASIL MAYONNAISE

1 small bunch fresh basil

1 cup vegan mayonnaise

1 clove garlic

1 tablespoon lemon juice

1 teaspoon salt

½ teaspoon black pepper

This crispy, unexpectedly gluten-free red veggie burger patty can be piled high with all your favorite toppings and a mayo you'll want to put on everything. Serve these burgers with fries and extra mayo for dipping.

« – »

1. Place beets into a large pot of boiling water and cook until tender to the center, about 30 minutes. Run under cool water and slip them out of their skins.

2. Preheat oven to 350°F.

3. In the bowl of a food processor, add beets and pulse until beets are smaller than peas but not mush. Stir in flour, bell pepper, garlic, onion, salt, pepper, and olive oil. Add more flour a few tablespoons at a time if mixture feels too wet or won't hold together in a ball.

4. Shape into 6 burger-sized patties and place on a greased baking sheet. Bake 25 minutes.

5. While burgers are baking, combine all mayonnaise ingredients in a food processor bowl. Process until the basil becomes flecks and the mayonnaise becomes pale green. Refrigerate until ready to use.

6. Place cooked beet patties on toasted whole-wheat (or gluten-free) buns and top with basil mayonnaise.

SAMOSA WRAP *with* GOLDEN RAISIN CHUTNEY

Everything you love about a spice-laden samosa without the frying! To make this for a crowd, prepare the filling and bake it in a casserole dish until hot. Serve with lots of pita on the side, and don't forget the chutney.

1. Place potatoes in a large pot of boiling water and cook until tender. Drain and set aside.

2. In a medium cast-iron pan, heat olive oil over medium heat, add coriander seed, garam masala, turmeric, salt, and pepper. Stir until fragrant, being careful not to burn the spices. Add ginger and garlic, and cook 1 more minute.

3. Stir potatoes into the spices and stir to coat. When potatoes are completely warmed through, remove pan from heat and add cilantro and peas.

4. Add all the chutney ingredients to a medium saucepan and bring to a boil, lower heat to medium, and allow to cook until thickened, about 15 minutes.

5. To assemble, place potato mixture onto lavash, roll and serve with warm chutney. Both filling and chutney are equally good the next day cold from the fridge.

» SERVES 6–8 «

4 large potatoes, peeled and chopped

2 tablespoons olive oil

1 teaspoon coriander seed

½ teaspoon garam masala

1 teaspoon turmeric

1 teaspoon salt

½ teaspoon black pepper

1 teaspoon grated ginger

2 cloves garlic, chopped

¼ cup chopped cilantro

½ cup frozen petite peas, cooked crisp tender

6–8 lavash flatbreads or tortillas

CHUTNEY

1 cup sugar

½ cup water

½ cup golden raisins

½ cup peeled and diced apple

¼ cup apple cider vinegar

1 medium jalapeño, seeded and finely chopped

¼ teaspoon turmeric

1 cinnamon stick

⅛ teaspoon allspice

⅛ teaspoon ground ginger

GRILLED PORTOBELLO SANDWICH *with* GARLICKY HORSERADISH MAYONNAISE

» SERVES 4 «

- ½ cup vegan mayonnaise
- 1 tablespoon prepared horseradish
- 1 teaspoon Dijon mustard
- 1 clove garlic, minced
- 2 tablespoons balsamic vinegar
- 1 tablespoon vegan Merlot wine
- 1 tablespoon vegan Worcestershire sauce
- 1 teaspoon salt
- 1 teaspoon black pepper
- 4 medium portobello mushrooms
- 3 tablespoons olive oil
- 4 French bread rolls
- 2 cups baby spinach

Portobello mushrooms have a magical quality that makes them feel and taste like meat, which means they're a good friend of most vegans. This hearty sandwich will satisfy any roast beef—like craving as well as deliver a horseradish zinger.

« – »

1. In a small bowl, mix together mayonnaise, horseradish, mustard, and garlic. Set aside.

2. In a shallow dish, combine balsamic vinegar, Merlot, Worcestershire sauce, salt, and pepper. Place portobello mushrooms in marinade, turning to coat. Let marinate 20 minutes on countertop, turning occasionally.

3. In a large grill pan or sauté pan over medium-high heat, sauté each portobello mushroom in olive oil about 3–4 minutes per side until tender. Remove from heat. Slice into ½" thick strips.

4. Split and toast French bread rolls, and spread a heaping teaspoonful of mayonnaise on each side. Top with spinach, divide mushrooms between the four sandwiches, and enjoy.

OPEN-FACED GRILLED VEGGIE SANDWICH *with* CREAMY PESTO

A sandwich piled high with veggies doesn't seem to qualify as junk food, but once you smear on creamy pesto and drizzle with sweetly acidic balsamic vinegar, it inches closer. No matter—this is quick to prepare and is plain delicious.

‹‹ – ››

1. In a small bowl, combine Basil Pesto with mayonnaise. Set aside.

2. Preheat oven to broil, or ready your barbecue, or heat a grill pan over medium-high heat.

3. In a large bowl, toss bell pepper, eggplant, and onion with oil, balsamic vinegar, salt, and pepper.

4. Cook bell pepper, eggplant, and onion using preferred method until vegetables are charred on each side and tender. Remove from heat and cook tomato slices, 1 minute on each side.

5. Toast baguette slightly just until crisp but not browned. Rub each slice with garlic and spread on a heaping tablespoonful of pesto mayonnaise.

6. Layer peppers, eggplant, onion, and tomato on top of each bread slice.

7. Drizzle with Balsamic Reduction and serve.

›› SERVES 4 ‹‹

1 recipe Basil Pesto (see Chapter 6)

½ cup vegan mayonnaise

1 medium red bell pepper, seeded and cut into thick planks

1 small eggplant, cut into ¼" rounds

1 medium red onion, peeled and sliced

2 tablespoons oil

1 tablespoon balsamic vinegar

1 teaspoon salt

½ teaspoon black pepper

1 large tomato, sliced thick

1 baguette, cut on the diagonal into 1" slices

2 cloves garlic

1 recipe Balsamic Reduction (see Chapter 6)

MESSY BARBECUE SANDWICH *with* TANGY SWEET MUSTARD RED POTATOES

2 teaspoons salt, divided

1 pound small red potatoes, cut in half

3 cups sweet and tangy vegan barbecue sauce

2 (8-ounce) packages tempeh, crumbled

1 medium onion, peeled and diced

1 tablespoon oil

½ cup vegan mayonnaise plus some to spread on sandwich

4 tablespoons raw agave

1 tablespoon Dijon mustard

1 tablespoon apple cider vinegar

½ teaspoon black pepper

4 French bread sandwich rolls, toasted

Curb your craving for barbecue with this vegan rendition. I always eat this sandwich with the potatoes, so I can't imagine one without the other. The tang of the mustard in the creamy textured potato salad perfectly complements the sweet and spicy sauce.

1. In a large stockpot, boil enough water and 1 teaspoon salt to cover potatoes. Cook potatoes about 15 minutes or until fork-tender. Drain.

2. In a medium saucepan, combine barbecue sauce and tempeh, and heat to a boil. Turn heat down to medium and let simmer.

3. In a small sauté pan over medium-high heat, sauté onions in oil until golden, stirring occasionally, about 10 minutes. Add to barbecue mixture. Remove from heat.

4. In a medium bowl, combine mayonnaise, agave, Dijon mustard, vinegar, remaining salt, and pepper. Toss potatoes in dressing.

5. On each toasted French bread roll, spread on mayonnaise and spoon on barbecue tempeh. Serve with red potatoes.

CHICKPEA TUNA MELT

Cross a garbanzo-bean base with some sea kelp, lemon juice, crunchy celery, and onion for the most mouthwatering mock tuna sandwich this side of the Atlantic. Serve the slightly briny sandwich open-faced on a fresh ciabatta roll to complete the mock experience.

1. Preheat oven to broil.

2. In a large bowl, lightly mash garbanzo beans to a coarse texture. Mix in celery, onion, mayonnaise, lemon juice, kelp granules, salt, and lemon pepper. Stir to combine completely.

3. Split ciabatta rolls and brush each cut side lightly with olive oil. Divide chickpea mixture between the four halves and top each half with ¼ cup cheese.

4. Broil until cheese is melted and bread is toasted, 4–5 minutes.

» SERVES 2 «

1 (15-ounce) can garbanzo beans (chickpeas), drained and rinsed

1 cup chopped celery

½ cup chopped red onion

1 cup vegan mayonnaise

1 tablespoon fresh-squeezed lemon juice

1 teaspoon kelp granules*

1 teaspoon salt

½ teaspoon lemon pepper

2 ciabatta rolls

Olive oil (for brushing)

1 cup vegan mozzarella shreds, divided

*NOTE: If you cannot find kelp granules, you can substitute with a 2" × 2" piece of nori or sushi roll sheet, chop it very finely with a knife, or run it through a coffee grinder to get a very fine chop.

PORTOBELLO CHEESESTEAK

- 1 pound portobello mushrooms
- 2 tablespoons oil, divided
- 1 teaspoon vegan Worcestershire sauce
- 1 teaspoon salt
- 1 teaspoon black pepper
- 1 medium green bell pepper, seeded and sliced
- 1 medium red bell pepper, seeded and sliced
- 1 medium onion, peeled and thinly sliced
- 4 sandwich rolls
- 2 cups vegan mozzarella shreds

A vegan take on the traditional cheesesteak: meaty to the tooth, the savory sautéed mushrooms mix with peppers and onions in a toasted roll to create a delicious sub. Top it with loads of cheese for melty goodness.

« – »

1. Preheat oven to broil.

2. Slice portobello mushrooms into ¼" slices. In a large bowl, toss mushrooms with 1 tablespoon oil, Worcestershire sauce, salt, and pepper.

3. In a medium sauté pan over medium-high heat, sauté mushrooms until tender. Remove from pan.

4. Add remaining tablespoon of oil to the pan and sauté peppers and onions until onions are golden and peppers are tender, about 8 minutes. Add mushrooms back to the pan and stir.

5. Spoon mushrooms and peppers into sandwich rolls; place ½ cup cheese on each. Place sandwiches under broiler and cook until cheese is melted and bread is toasted, about 4–5 minutes.

EGGPLANT BLTA *with* GARLIC CHIVE MAYO

» SERVES 4 «

1 cup vegan mayonnaise

1 clove garlic, pressed

2 tablespoons minced chives

1 teaspoon salt

½ teaspoon black pepper

8 slices sourdough bread

1 recipe Eggplant Bacon (see Chapter 1), or 1 (15-ounce) package of Lightlife Smart Bacon, cooked

1 medium tomato, sliced

6–8 leaves butter leaf lettuce

1 medium ripe avocado, sliced

When you think of comfort food, it doesn't get much better than the BLT. Make this one with Eggplant Bacon (see Chapter 1), avocado, and garlicky mayo for a vegan version that raises the bar on the original.

1. In a small bowl, combine mayonnaise with garlic (to press garlic, use a garlic press or mash with the side of a heavy knife), chives, salt, and pepper.

2. Toast sourdough bread until golden and place about ½ tablespoon garlic mayonnaise on each slice.

3. Pile on Eggplant Bacon, tomato, lettuce, avocado, and more salt and pepper if desired, close sandwich and enjoy.

BARBECUED TEMPEH WRAP

» SERVES 4 «

1 cup barbecue sauce

1 (8-ounce) package tempeh, crumbled

4 whole-wheat tortillas or lavash flatbread

4 tablespoons vegan mayonnaise

2 cups mesclun greens

1 medium green apple, cored and sliced thin

½ medium red onion, peeled and sliced thin

¼ cup chopped fresh cilantro

1 recipe Creamy Ranch Dressing (see Chapter 6)

This sandwich is a favorite with my catering clients—who range from students to rock stars, so that's saying a lot! This takes no more than 10 minutes to assemble, so it's perfect for when you need to eat fast. Resist leaving out any of the ingredients. They work in harmony, creating a most mouthwatering wrap.

1. In a medium bowl, mix barbecue sauce and crumbled tempeh.

2. For each wrap, spread on a tablespoon of mayonnaise, ¼ of the barbecue tempeh, ½ cup mesclun greens, ¼ of the apple slices, ¼ of the onion slices, and a sprinkle of cilantro.

3. Drizzle on Creamy Ranch Dressing. Wrap and devour!

BACON EGG SALAD

Vegan bacon gives a salty tang to this salad, which features tofu and garbanzo beans masquerading as eggs. French bread croutons add the crunch required in any self-respecting junk food.

» SERVES 3–4 «

1. Preheat oven to 350°F. Line a baking sheet with parchment paper.

2. In a medium bowl, toss French bread cubes with olive oil. Place on prepared baking sheet. Bake croutons until golden brown and crunchy, about 8 minutes, tossing halfway through to toast evenly. Remove from oven.

3. In a large bowl, slightly mash garbanzo beans. Mix in tofu.

4. In a small bowl, stir together relish, mayonnaise, Dijon mustard, bacon, salt, and pepper. Add to tofu mixture along with the croutons and stir to combine.

5. Serve large scoops on butter leaf lettuce if desired.

- 2 cups French bread, cut into 2" cubes
- 2 tablespoons olive oil
- 1 (15-ounce) can garbanzo beans, drained and rinsed
- 4 ounces firm tofu, drained and chopped into ¼" dice
- 2 tablespoons pickle relish
- ¾ cup vegan mayonnaise
- 1 tablespoon Dijon mustard
- 1 (6-ounce) package Lightlife Smart Bacon, chopped
- 1 teaspoon salt
- ½ teaspoon black pepper
- 6–8 leaves butter leaf lettuce (optional)

VEGAN CRAB CAKE BURGER

Serve this at a party with a spicy remoulade or on a bun with burger accompaniments.

» SERVES 4 «

1. In a food processor, pulse hearts of palm into ½" bits.

2. To a large bowl, add flaked hearts of palm, ½ cup bread crumbs, and remaining ingredients except for oil. Stir to combine ingredients.

3. Shape mixture into 4 patties and dredge in remaining bread crumbs. At this point, the cakes can be refrigerated overnight or frozen for later use.

4. In a medium heavy-bottomed sauté pan over medium-high heat, add cooking oil and fry patties on each side until golden, about 3 minutes on each side. Serve immediately on soft rolls.

- 1 (14-ounce) can hearts of palm, drained
- 2 cups bread crumbs, divided
- 1 medium red bell pepper, seeded and chopped
- 2 ribs celery, chopped
- ¼ cup minced onion
- ¼ cup vegan mayonnaise
- 1 teaspoon Dijon mustard
- 2 teaspoons chopped fresh dill
- 1 teaspoon nori sprinkles
- 1 teaspoon salt
- ½ teaspoon black pepper
- 4 tablespoons oil (for frying)

MEATBALL SUBWICH

2 cups water

1 (8-ounce) package tempeh, crumbled

2 tablespoons ground flaxseeds

¼ cup water

½ cup chopped onion

1 teaspoon oil

1 clove garlic, chopped

1 tablespoon tomato paste

1 teaspoon vegan Worcester-shire sauce

1 teaspoon light soy sauce

½ cup bread crumbs

½ cup finely minced walnuts

½ teaspoon dried oregano

½ teaspoon dried parsley

½ teaspoon dried basil

4 French bread rolls

2 cups marinara sauce

1 cup vegan mozzarella shreds

If you're in a rush, you can use store-bought vegan meatballs, but it's simple enough to make them from scratch, and they taste way better. Onion, garlic, walnuts, and herbs are the stars of these tempeh-based meatballs. Wedge them into a slab of French bread, smother in marinara, and top with a mini mountain of cheese for lunch nirvana.

« – »

1. Preheat oven to 350°F. Line a baking sheet with parchment paper.

2. Bring 2 cups water to a boil under a steamer basket. Add crumbled tempeh. Cover and let steam 10 minutes or until pliable.

3. In a small bowl, mix flaxseeds with ¼ cup water and set aside.

4. In a medium sauté pan over medium heat, cook onions in oil, stirring until translucent, about 3 minutes. Add garlic and sauté 1 more minute. Remove from heat.

5. In a large bowl, combine all the remaining ingredients (except rolls, marinara sauce, and cheese) with the flaxseeds, tempeh, and onions and mix with hands until very well com-bined. If the mixture is too dry to be shaped into a ball, add 1 more tablespoon tomato paste. If mixture is too wet, add bread crumbs ¼ cup at a time until you can easily shape into 1½" balls.

6. Place meatballs on prepared baking sheet.

7. Bake 25–30 minutes, carefully turning meatballs halfway through cooking. Meatballs are done when they turn a deep golden brown. Set oven to broil.

8. Open French bread roll without separating two halves, place four or five meatballs in each roll, spoon on ½ cup marinara sauce, and top each with ¼ cup cheese.

9. Place sandwiches under broiler until cheese is melted and bread is toasted, about 5 minutes.

CHICKEN SALAD with WALNUTS, APPLES, and CELERY

To cook nonvegan versions of classic junk food, you need to become familiar with such ingredients as vegan chicken bouillon and TVP (textured vegetable protein), both of which are featured here. The bouillon imparts a "chickeny" flavor sans actual chicken, and TVP has a texture that mimics the mouth-feel of the meat. Try Bob's Red Mill brand—they make a mean TVP.

----

1. In a medium saucepan over high heat, bring vegetable broth and chicken bouillon base to a vigorous boil. Place TVP in a heatproof bowl and add hot liquid mixture, let sit 10 minutes. Drain, reserving liquid. When cool enough to touch, place TVP in a kitchen towel and squeeze out excess liquid.

2. In a medium bowl, combine mayonnaise, salt, pepper, Dijon mustard, celery, red onion, walnuts, and apple. Stir in TVP.

3. Serve on split ciabatta rolls with lettuce and extra mayonnaise.

›› SERVES 4 ‹‹

- 2 cups vegetable broth
- 1 teaspoon vegan chicken bouillon base
- ½ cup small-grain TVP
- 1 cup vegan mayonnaise plus some for spreading on bread
- 1 teaspoon salt
- ½ teaspoon black pepper
- 2 teaspoons Dijon mustard
- ½ cup finely chopped celery
- ¼ cup finely chopped red onion
- ¼ cup chopped walnuts
- 1 medium apple, cored and chopped
- 4 ciabatta sandwich rolls
- 3–4 green leaf lettuce leaves

PAD THAI WRAP

1 (8-ounce) package flat rice
    noodles

1 teaspoon oil

1 (6-ounce) package savory
    baked tofu, teriyaki flavor

¼ cup soy sauce

3 tablespoons lemon juice

1 tablespoon brown sugar

1 teaspoon chili paste

2 tablespoons peanut oil

1 medium onion, peeled and
    thinly sliced

2 cloves garlic, chopped

1 red chili, sliced

3 green onions, green and
    white parts, cut thinly on
    the diagonal

¼ cup chopped peanuts

¼ cup finely chopped cilantro

6 tortillas or flatbread

3 cups mesclun greens

1 recipe Spicy Peanut Sauce
    (see Chapter 6)

When Asian food is all you crave, you'll want to whip up these savory-sweet wraps. They include the five essential junk food groups: carbs (noodles), meat (teriyaki tofu), sugar, spice (red chili), and peanuts. Sayonara, takeout!

« – »

1. In a large saucepan, boil enough water to cover noodles, add noodles, and cook about 10 minutes or until tender. Drain. Toss in 1 teaspoon oil to prevent noodles from sticking together.

2. Slice tofu into thin strips.

3. In a small bowl, combine soy sauce, lemon juice, brown sugar, and chili paste. Set aside.

4. In a large sauté pan over high heat, coat pan with peanut oil and sauté onion, garlic, and red chili until onions are translucent, about 3–4 minutes. Add noodles, tofu strips, and green onion. Toss with tongs to mix well. Add soy sauce mixture. Stir well. Remove from heat. Stir in peanuts and cilantro.

5. On each tortilla or flatbread, place about ½ cup Pad Thai, ½ cup mesclun greens, and drizzle on Spicy Peanut Sauce. Wrap into a cylinder, secure with a toothpick in two places, and cut in half.

CAESAR SALAD CHICKEN WRAP

Drench this wrap with the creamy, delicious dressing and devour.

- 1 head romaine, washed, dried, torn into pieces
- ¾ cup Caesar Salad Dressing (see Chapter 6), divided
- 4 whole-wheat tortillas or lavash flatbread
- 1 (9-ounce) package Beyond Meat Beyond Chicken Strips
- 1 medium tomato, sliced
- ½ medium red onion, peeled and thinly sliced

1. In a large bowl, toss lettuce with about ½ cup dressing.

2. On each tortilla, spread a few teaspoons of Caesar Salad Dressing and add a large handful of lettuce, then top with chicken strips, tomatoes, and onions.

3. Wrap tightly and cut in half.

TOFU LETTUCE WRAP *with* PEANUT SAUCE

Here's the vegan version of the popular lettuce wraps you find in restaurants. Firm tofu works best in this recipe, as it holds up to being sautéed without crumbling.

- 1 (14-ounce) package firm tofu, drained and cubed
- 1 tablespoon oil
- 2 cloves garlic, chopped
- 1 tablespoon minced ginger
- 1–2 medium red chilies, seeded and sliced
- 1 teaspoon sesame oil
- ½ cup soy sauce
- 1 tablespoon hoisin sauce
- ½ cup shredded carrots
- ½ cup shredded cabbage
- ½ cup bean sprouts
- 3 green onions, cut thinly
- ¼ cup finely chopped cilantro
- Juice of 2 medium limes
- 6–8 leaves butter leaf lettuce
- 1 recipe Spicy Peanut Sauce (see Chapter 6)

1. In a large sauté pan over medium-high heat, sauté tofu in oil 15 minutes until golden. Add garlic, ginger, red chilies, sesame oil, soy sauce, and hoisin sauce. Cook until sauce comes to a boil. Remove from heat.

2. In a large bowl, combine carrots, cabbage, bean sprouts, green onions, cilantro, and lime juice.

3. On each leaf of butter lettuce, put a heaping tablespoonful of cabbage mixture topped with a heaping tablespoon of tofu mixture. Drizzle with Spicy Peanut Sauce.

CRISPY CHICKEN RANCH BURGER

1 cup ice water

1½ cups all-purpose flour

1 teaspoon baking powder

1 teaspoon salt

½ teaspoon black pepper

Canola oil (for frying)

1 (16-ounce) package firm tofu, drained and cut through the width of the block, making 4 patties

1 recipe Creamy Ranch Dressing (see Chapter 6)

4 hamburger buns

1 medium ripe avocado, sliced

4 leaves lettuce

½ medium onion, peeled and thinly sliced

1 medium tomato, sliced

Fry up those slices of tofu with a tempura batter for a delicious sandwich. Be sure to drench these delicious patties with a generous helping of Creamy Ranch Dressing to complete the deep-fried feast.

« – »

1. In a medium bowl, combine ice water, flour, baking powder, salt, and pepper, and stir until just combined; a few lumps are fine.

2. In a deep 2-quart pot, heat enough oil to submerge tofu patties over medium-high heat. You'll know the oil is hot enough when bubbles appear around the base of a chopstick inserted into the oil.

3. Dip tofu patties into the tempura batter, turning to completely coat, and carefully place patties in the heated oil. Fry about 1–2 minutes, turning when light golden brown, then fry the second side 1–2 minutes longer. Set on paper towels to drain. Repeat for all four patties.

4. Spoon a tablespoon of Creamy Ranch Dressing on buns and add tofu patty. Garnish with avocado, lettuce, onion, tomato, and extra Creamy Ranch Dressing.

BLACK BEAN BURGER *with* ONION RINGS

This burger is made extra "junky" with the addition of those deliciously salty and crunchy canned fried onion strips. You know the ones: they're in the same family as canned potato sticks. In any case, mix 'em in for extra kick. If you have time, pair with homemade beer-battered onion rings for a totally amazing combo.

« – »

1. In a large bowl, mash black beans with a potato masher until they are coarsely chopped but not mushy. Add bread crumbs, fried onions, mayonnaise, cilantro, salt, pepper, garlic powder, barbecue sauce, ketchup, and chili powder. Mix by hand until all ingredients are combined.

2. Shape by hand into patties. If burgers stick to your hands, add ½ cup bread crumbs; if burgers don't hold together, add 2 tablespoons mayonnaise.

3. On a grill pan or 10" heavy skillet over medium-high heat, cook each burger in a teaspoon of oil about 4–5 minutes on each side. Patties can also be baked on a parchment-lined cookie sheet in a 375°F oven for 25 minutes, turning patties halfway through cooking.

4. Place each patty on a toasted hamburger bun with mayonnaise, barbecue sauce, ketchup, and pickles as garnishes. If you desire, top with two onion rings.

» SERVES 4 «

- 1 (15-ounce) can black beans, drained and rinsed
- ¾ cup bread crumbs
- 1 cup canned French's Crispy Fried Onions, crushed
- 2 tablespoons vegan mayonnaise
- 2 tablespoons finely chopped cilantro
- 1 teaspoon salt
- ½ teaspoon black pepper
- ½ teaspoon garlic powder
- 1 tablespoon barbecue sauce
- 1 tablespoon ketchup
- 1 teaspoon chili powder
- Oil (for cooking)
- 4 hamburger buns, toasted
- Vegan mayonnaise, barbecue sauce, ketchup, and pickles (for garnish)

SLOPPY JOES

Put this dish up against the meat version of a sloppy joe in a taste test, and I'd bet most wouldn't be able to tell the difference—they're amazingly similar in flavor and texture.

« - »

1. In a large sauté pan over medium-high heat, sauté onions and carrots in oil until onions are translucent. Add garlic to pan and cook 1 minute.

2. Add salt, pepper, brown sugar, balsamic vinegar, Worcestershire sauce, tomato paste, and tomato sauce, stirring well. Add broth and lentils and bring to a boil. Turn heat down to medium and cook 5 minutes.

3. Spoon mixture onto toasted buns and serve while hot.

>> SERVES 4 <<

- ½ medium onion, peeled and chopped
- ¼ cup finely chopped carrot
- 1 tablespoon oil
- 1 clove garlic, chopped
- 1 teaspoon salt
- ½ teaspoon black pepper
- 2 tablespoons brown sugar
- 2 teaspoons balsamic vinegar
- 1 teaspoon vegan Worcestershire sauce
- 4 tablespoons tomato paste
- 1 cup tomato sauce
- ½ cup vegetable broth
- 1 cup cooked brown lentils
- 4 hamburger buns, toasted

CURRY MUSHROOM BURGER *with* MANGO CHUTNEY

- 6 ounces button mushrooms, chopped
- ½ medium onion, peeled and chopped
- 1 clove garlic, chopped
- 1 tablespoon canola oil
- 1 teaspoon salt
- ½ teaspoon black pepper
- 1 cup cooked chickpeas
- ¾ cup vegan mayonnaise
- 3 teaspoons curry powder, divided
- 2 tablespoons finely chopped cilantro
- 2 cups bread crumbs
- Oil (for frying)
- ½ cup vegan mayonnaise
- 1 teaspoon chili sauce
- 4 sandwich rolls
- 1 (8-ounce) jar mango chutney

Enjoy a taste of India, without needing to find the takeout menu or tip the delivery person. The classic junk combo of spicy and savory-sweet flavors is on display here: chickpeas supply the savory; mango chutney supplies the sweet.

« — — — — — — — — — — — — — — — — — — — »

1. In a medium sauté pan over medium-high heat, sauté mushrooms, onion, and garlic in oil until onions are translucent, about 3–4 minutes. Add salt and pepper. Remove from heat.

2. In food processor, add chickpeas and pulse until very coarsely chopped. Add mayonnaise, 2 teaspoons curry powder, cilantro, and half of mushroom mixture, leaving behind any liquid. Pour into a large bowl and add 1 cup bread crumbs.

3. Form into patties and coat with remaining bread crumbs.

4. Heat a large sauté pan over medium-high heat, adding 1 teaspoon of oil per patty. Cook patties 3–5 minutes or until golden brown, flip and cook another 3–5 minutes.

5. In a small bowl, combine mayonnaise, 1 teaspoon curry powder, and chili sauce.

6. On each roll, spread a teaspoonful of curry mayonnaise and mango chutney. Top with a curry chickpea patty.

BUFFALO SLIDERS *with* CREAMY RANCH DRESSING

Cauliflower is proving its versatility yet again as the base of this classically flavored dish. Don't skimp on the celery unless you want your mouth to burn off— it supplies a cool crunch to counter the five-alarm sauce.

« - »

1. Preheat oven to 375°F.

2. Mix Creamy Ranch Dressing and celery.

3. In a medium bowl, whisk together water, flour, and salt until smooth. Dip each piece of cauliflower in the batter and place on a greased baking sheet. Bake 25 minutes, turning once halfway through.

4. In a small saucepan over medium-high heat, bring hot sauce to a boil, then remove from heat. Dip baked cauliflower into sauce and set aside on a plate.

5. To assemble, place a heaping teaspoonful of ranch-celery mixture on the bottom bun of each sandwich. Add onion, lettuce, and tomato. Top with cauliflower and cap with bun.

6. Serve with extra ranch-celery mixture and heated hot sauce on the side.

1 recipe Creamy Ranch Dressing (see Chapter 6)

1 cup finely chopped celery

1 cup water

1 cup flour

1 teaspoon salt

1 head cauliflower, cut into florets

1 cup Frank's RedHot sauce

6 slider buns or 6 hot dog buns cut into thirds

½ medium red onion, peeled and sliced

1 cup shredded lettuce

1 medium Roma tomato, sliced

SOUTHWEST SLIDERS *with* SPICY QUESO SAUCE

1 clove garlic, minced

½ medium onion, peeled and
chopped

1 tablespoon oil plus extra for
frying

4 tablespoons flour

2 cups nondairy milk

2 cups vegan Cheddar shreds

1 (15-ounce) can diced
tomatoes with green chilies

1 medium jalapeño, seeded
and chopped

½ cup chopped red bell pepper

½ cup chopped onion

½ cup bread crumbs

½ cup cooked brown rice

½ cup pinto beans, cooked and
mashed

½ cup yam, cooked and
mashed

1 teaspoon salt

½ teaspoon black pepper

1 teaspoon chili powder

1 teaspoon cumin

½ teaspoon garlic powder

Mini burger buns or hot dog
buns cut into thirds

You can buy vegan queso, but since it's such a
breeze to make your own, why bother? Break out the
bibs when you sit down to devour these delectable
nuggets—it's a messy endeavor!

« - »

1. In a medium saucepan over medium heat, sauté garlic and
onion in oil until onions are translucent, about 3–4 minutes.
Add flour to the pan, stirring with a whisk, and cook 1 minute.
Add milk and stir until mixture thickens. Add vegan Cheddar
shreds and 1 cup diced tomatoes with chilies, drained. Bring
to a boil, then turn heat to low, and let simmer while burgers
cook.

2. In a medium sauté pan over medium heat, sauté jalapeño,
red peppers, and onions in oil until onions are translucent,
about 3–4 minutes. Remove from heat.

3. In a large bowl, combine cooked onion mixture, diced
tomatoes with chilies, bread crumbs, brown rice, beans, yam,
salt, pepper, chili powder, cumin, and garlic powder until well
mixed. Using hands, form into 3" patties.

4. In a large sauté or grill pan over medium-high heat, sauté
burgers in a few teaspoons of oil 3–5 minutes on each side.

5. Remove prepared queso sauce from heat.

6. Place cooked burgers on bun bottoms, spoon queso sauce
over the patties, and cover with bun tops.

CHAPTER 3

Comfort Food Meets Takeout

• Tempting No-Meat Entrées •

CHICKEN POT PIE

The homemade Savory Pie Crust is what makes this so flipping fantastic, so resist the urge to use an inferior store-bought kind. The creamy filling that holds the goodies (a.k.a. veggies and chicken) in this epic crust tastes so rich you may be tempted to eat it on its own by the spoonful.

1 recipe Savory Pie Crust (see this page)
½ cup diced carrots
½ cup diced celery
½ cup diced potato
1 small onion, peeled and chopped
1 clove garlic, chopped
4 tablespoons vegan butter
½ cup flour
2 cups vegetable broth
1 cup nondairy milk
½ cup nutritional yeast
½ cup frozen peas
1 cup chopped chicken strips, such as Beyond Meat Beyond Chicken Strips Grilled, or 1 cup cooked chickpeas
1 teaspoon celery salt
½ teaspoon black pepper

1. Preheat oven to 350°F.

2. On a lightly floured surface, roll one disk of Savory Pie Crust dough to fit into a 2-quart baking dish. Roll the other disk to fit on top.

3. In a medium sauté pan over medium-high heat, sauté carrots, celery, potato, onion, and garlic in butter until vegetables are tender, about 10 minutes.

4. Add flour to the sautéed vegetables, then stir, cooking 1 more minute.

5. Whisk broth and milk slowly into sauté pan and cook until bubbly and thick. Add nutritional yeast, peas, chicken, celery salt, and pepper.

6. Pour into prepared baking dish. Top with remaining dough. Crimp edges to seal. Cut four small vent holes in top crust.

7. Bake 45–50 minutes. Allow to cool slightly before digging in!

Savory Pie Crust

3½ cups flour
1½ teaspoons salt
⅔ cup vegan butter, chilled
3 tablespoons olive oil
3 tablespoons ice water

1. In a food processor with the blade fitting attached, pulse flour and salt, adding butter 1 tablespoon at a time until mixture resembles coarse meal. Alternatively, use a pastry blender or two knives to cut butter into the flour.

2. Pour in olive oil and pulse.

3. Pour in ice water 1 tablespoon at a time until a spoonful of dough can be formed into a ball that doesn't crumble. Do not overmix.

4. If not using immediately, wrap tightly in plastic wrap and refrigerate or freeze.

KALE *and* CHEESE TORTELLINI *in* SAGE BUTTER

» SERVES 4 «

- 1 bunch kale, deveined and minced
- ½ medium onion, peeled and minced
- 1 clove garlic, minced
- 2 tablespoons olive oil
- 1 teaspoon salt
- ¼ teaspoon ground nutmeg
- 4 ounces vegan cheese, such as Field Roast Creamy Original Chao Slices, chopped
- 1 (12-ounce) package square or circular wonton wrappers
- 3 fresh sage leaves, chopped
- 2 tablespoons vegan butter
- ½ teaspoon salt
- ¼ teaspoon white pepper

You can find the wonton wrappers for this recipe in the refrigerated section of your well-stocked grocery store—just look for nonvegan ingredients. Rely on *YouTube*, as I did, for a visual on how to create the tortellini shape.

« – »

1. In a large sauté pan over medium heat, sauté kale, onion, and garlic in oil until very tender. Add salt, nutmeg, and cheese. Set aside off the heat.

2. Get out your smart device and search for a video on how to wrap the tortellini. You'll want to use about a teaspoon of kale filling in the center of each wonton wrapper; using more will make wrapping much harder. If the tortellini shape confounds you, don't worry. You can fold each wrapper in half over the filling using some water to seal the edge.

3. Once you have all the tortellini shapes done, place them in a large stockpot full of boiling salted water. Give them an initial stir to prevent sticking and cook 4 minutes or until they are floating. Drain gently to retain shape.

4. In a large sauté pan over medium-high heat, fry sage in butter until very fragrant. Add cooked tortellini to the pan and swirl around in butter. Sprinkle on salt and white pepper. Serve immediately.

RED POTATO SALAD *with* DILL, CHIVES, *and* DIJON MAYO DRESSING

In my mind, potato salad is an entire class of comfort food all on its own. This version with its fresh herbs and tangy dressing really stands out. It's perfect to take to a barbecue or beach picnic.

‹‹ – ››

1. In a large stockpot, boil potatoes in salted water until tender, about 15 minutes. Drain well.

2. While the potatoes cook, combine the remaining ingredients in a medium bowl to make the dressing.

3. In a large bowl, combine the hot potatoes with the dressing and bring to room temperature. Refrigerate, serve cold.

>> SERVES 8 <<

6 cups cubed red potatoes

¼ cup chopped green onions

¼ cup chopped celery

1 clove garlic, minced

1 teaspoon salt

½ teaspoon black pepper

1 teaspoon fresh dill

2 tablespoons chopped chives

¼ cup vegan mayonnaise

1 tablespoon Dijon mustard

2 tablespoons olive oil

1 tablespoon apple cider vinegar

CAULIFLOWER PICCATA

Lemon and capers are classic culinary best friends, and when you add the unmatchable duo of butter and wine to a grilled cauliflower steak, it's a veggie lovefest on a plate.

‹‹ – ››

1. Drizzle olive oil over cauliflower slabs, add salt and pepper. Grill over medium-low heat 6 minutes on each side. Alternatively, you can roast in a 400°F oven 15 minutes, turning once halfway through.

2. Make the sauce: In a large sauté pan over medium-high heat, cook butter and olive oil until very hot and sizzling. Add lemon juice, vegetable broth, wine, capers, salt, and pepper. Whisk until reduced by half, about 5 minutes.

3. Place cauliflower on plates, top with sauce and parsley.

>> SERVES 4 <<

2 tablespoons olive oil

1 head cauliflower, cut 1" slabs

1 teaspoon salt

½ teaspoon black pepper

SAUCE

2 tablespoons vegan butter

2 tablespoons olive oil

3 tablespoons lemon juice

¼ cup vegetable broth

¼ cup vegan dry white wine

4 tablespoons capers, drained

½ teaspoon salt

¼ teaspoon black pepper

2 tablespoons chopped parsley

LAYERED EGGPLANT PARMESAN CASSEROLE

» SERVES 6 «

2 cups bread crumbs

1 tablespoon nutritional yeast

1 teaspoon salt

1 teaspoon oregano

1 teaspoon parsley

1 cup nondairy milk

½ cup cornstarch

2 tablespoons oil (for frying)

1 large eggplant, sliced into ¼" rounds

2 cups vegan mozzarella shreds

1 recipe Vegan Ricotta (see Chapter 6)

3 cups marinara sauce

You had me at "casserole," because there's not much that's junkier than throwing everything into a big ol' dish and baking it until the flavors are all melded and melty and messy and mouthwatering.

« – »

1. Preheat oven to 350°F. Lightly grease a 9" × 13" baking dish.

2. In a shallow dish, combine bread crumbs, nutritional yeast, salt, oregano, and parsley.

3. In a second shallow dish, pour in milk.

4. In a third shallow bowl, add cornstarch.

5. In a large sauté pan over medium-high heat, heat oil.

6. Dredge each piece of eggplant in cornstarch, then milk, then coat with bread crumb mixture.

7. Fry in heated oil until golden brown on both sides, about 5–7 minutes.

8. Place ⅓ of cooked eggplant in a single layer in the bottom of prepared baking dish. Top with ½ cup cheese, ⅓ of the Vegan Ricotta, and 1 cup marinara. Continue layering, topping with cheese shreds.

9. Bake 45 minutes. Let cool 10 minutes before serving.

CELLOPHANE NOODLES *with* SHIITAKE MUSHROOMS

I love noodles, but sometimes they seem to require a lot of time and an elaborate recipe. This recipe is fast, because the noodles don't require much more than a warm bath, and delightfully flavorful, because of: mushrooms.

«‒ »

1. In a large bowl, pour hot water to cover noodles and allow to soak 10 minutes before draining.

2. In a large sauté pan over medium-high heat, add mushrooms, carrots, onion, ginger, and olive oil and cook until sizzling, about 5 minutes.

3. Pour in broth and cook until broth has mostly evaporated, about 5 minutes. Using tongs, add noodles to pan and stir.

4. Serve with a drizzle of sesame oil and top with chopped green onion.

» SERVES 4 «

1 (6-ounce) package cellophane (bean thread) noodles

2 cups sliced shiitake mushrooms

½ cup matchstick carrots

½ cup sliced onion

1 tablespoon minced ginger

2 tablespoons olive oil

1 cup vegetable broth

1 teaspoon sesame oil

¼ cup chopped green onion

MAC and CHEESE BAKE

I could eat this every day of my life and die an incredibly happy woman. This is the ultimate carb-load comfort food, featuring pasta, bread crumbs, vegan Cheddar shreds, nutritional yeast, butter, and milk. It technically serves six, but if you're like me, you could easily polish off an entire recipe all by yourself.

» SERVES 6 «

½ cup nondairy milk

1 recipe Cheese Sauce (see Chapter 6)

1 pound elbow pasta, cooked

½ cup vegan Cheddar shreds

½ cup bread crumbs

¼ cup walnuts, finely ground

¼ cup nutritional yeast

2 tablespoons vegan butter, melted

1. Preheat oven to 350°F. Lightly grease a 9" × 13" baking dish.

2. In a large saucepan over medium heat, whisk milk into the Cheese Sauce. When heated through, add cooked pasta, stirring to combine thoroughly.

3. Pour into prepared baking dish. Top with cheese shreds.

4. In a small bowl, combine bread crumbs, walnuts, nutritional yeast, and butter, and mix well. Evenly sprinkle over cheese layer.

5. Bake 25 minutes or until top is golden brown. Waste no time devouring.

BROCCOLI CHEESE SOUP

½ cup chopped carrot

¼ cup chopped onion

4 tablespoons vegan butter

¼ cup flour

6 cups vegetable broth

2 cups chopped broccoli

¼ teaspoon ground nutmeg

1 teaspoon salt

½ teaspoon black pepper

1 cup shredded vegan Cheddar cheese, such as Follow Your Heart brand

2 cups almond milk

¼ teaspoon smoked paprika

Yum! This soup covers a lot of bases—it's creamy, cheesy, and comforting. It also freezes well and tastes great the next day for lunch if you're lucky enough to have leftovers.

« – »

1. In a medium saucepan over medium-high heat, cook carrot and onion in butter until onion is translucent, about 3–4 minutes. Add flour to the pan and whisk to incorporate butter into flour. Continue whisking until flour begins to turn golden.

2. Whisk as you add vegetable broth to the pan. Turn heat to low and cook 10 minutes.

3. At this point, you can purée the base of the soup in two batches while being careful not to overfill your blender; if you don't mind the chunks of carrot and onion you can skip this step.

4. Add remaining ingredients except paprika to the pan and cook, stirring often, another 10 minutes or until broccoli is tender. Top with paprika before serving.

CHILE RELLEÑOS CASSEROLE

Adding vinegar to soy milk is a vegan trick for creating a "sour" milk (similar to the tangy flavor of buttermilk). For a taste of Mexico, this recipe satisfies—serve with a piping-hot side of Tex-Mex Corn Bread (see Chapter 4).

1 cup soy milk

1 teaspoon apple cider vinegar

1 (8-ounce) container vegan cream cheese

4 cups vegan Cheddar shreds

8 canned whole green chilies, drained and rinsed

1 cup flour

3 tablespoons nutritional yeast

1½ teaspoons baking soda

2 teaspoons baking powder

½ teaspoon salt

⅛ teaspoon turmeric

1. Preheat oven to 375°F. Lightly grease a 9" × 9" baking dish.

2. In a small bowl, mix soy milk and apple cider vinegar, then set aside.

3. In a medium bowl, mix cream cheese and cheese shreds until well combined. Make a small slit at the top of each chili and stuff with ⅛ of the cheese filling. Lay stuffed chilies in prepared baking dish.

4. In a medium bowl with a whisk, stir flour, nutritional yeast, baking soda, baking powder, salt, and turmeric. Stir in soy milk-vinegar mixture. Pour into a blender and mix on high speed 1 minute.

5. Pour over chilies.

6. Bake 25 minutes or until batter is set and golden brown. Buen provecho!

SOUTH-of-the-BORDER POTATO TACOS

» SERVES 3-4 «

1 pound baking potatoes, peeled and chopped into 2" pieces

2 teaspoons salt, divided

¼ cup diced onion

1 medium jalapeño, seeded and chopped finely

1 tablespoon plus 2 teaspoons oil, divided

1 teaspoon cumin

¼ cup chopped cilantro plus more for garnish

¼ cup nutritional yeast

½ cup vegan mozzarella shreds

6 corn tortillas

1 recipe Avocado Sauce (see Chapter 6)

A cheesy, caliente potato taco is delicious. A cheesy, caliente potato taco that's fried is outta this world. You should serve creamy Avocado Sauce on the side (better just make a really big batch).

« – »

1. In a medium pot, boil potatoes in 1 teaspoon salt until tender, then drain.

2. In a medium sauté pan over medium-high heat, cook onion and jalapeño in 2 teaspoons oil until onion is translucent, about 4 minutes, then add cumin.

3. Turn heat down to low and add potatoes, remaining salt, cilantro, nutritional yeast, and cheese. Mash potatoes slightly, stirring to combine all ingredients. Cook 2–3 minutes. Remove from heat.

4. In a dry 10" skillet over medium-high heat, place tortillas in the pan one at a time, heating on each side a few seconds, just long enough to soften. Wrap tortillas in a kitchen towel to keep warm.

5. Fill each tortilla with 2 heaping tablespoonfuls of potato mixture and fold.

6. Add 1 tablespoon oil to pan and cook each tortilla on each side until crispy.

7. Garnish with extra cilantro. Serve with Avocado Sauce on the side.

JACKFRUIT TACOS

2 tablespoons oil

½ cup chopped onion

1 (14-ounce) can green
jackfruit in brine, drained

1 tablespoon vegan
Worcestershire sauce

1 teaspoon salt

½ teaspoon black pepper

1 small onion, peeled and
chopped

¼ cup chopped cilantro

12 corn tortillas

1 recipe Avocado Sauce
(see Chapter 6)

This vegan street taco features jackfruit sautéed with onion until it's deep golden brown and oh-so-flavorful. Worcestershire sauce is the secret ingredient that gives this a salty-meaty kick. Finish by drizzling (or drenching) with creamy-cooling Avocado Sauce.

1. In a medium sauté pan over medium-high heat, heat oil and sauté ½ cup onion until golden brown. Add jackfruit and cook 8–10 minutes, adding more oil if needed to keep from sticking. Add Worcestershire sauce, salt, and pepper to pan and cook 2 more minutes. Remove from heat.

2. In a small bowl, mix onion and cilantro.

3. In a large dry sauté pan over medium heat, cook corn tortillas just until they turn soft, about 30 seconds on each side, and keep wrapped in a towel.

4. Spoon a heaping tablespoonful of jackfruit onto each tortilla; add a teaspoonful of onion-cilantro mixture. Serve with Avocado Sauce.

TEMPEH FAJITAS

Break out the grill pan, folks. It's time to make fajitas, and delectable breaded tempeh fajitas at that. The Easy Salsa Fresca is pretty healthy and tastes great as a topping, but if you're on a true junk food bender, I understand if you opt to omit.

« – » »

1. In a small shallow dish, mix flour, chili powder, salt, garlic powder, onion, cumin, lime juice, and 1 tablespoon olive oil. Add tempeh, turning to coat, and let marinate at least 1 hour on countertop.

2. In a large grill pan or sauté pan over medium-high heat, cook onions and peppers in 1 teaspoon olive oil until onions are charred on one side, about 5 minutes in the grill pan, or sauté until golden and tender crisp. Remove peppers and onions to a serving plate.

3. Add tempeh and 1 teaspoon olive oil to the pan and cook until tempeh becomes slightly crispy and browned. Place on serving plate with peppers and onions.

4. In a dry 10" skillet over medium-high heat, warm each tortilla until soft and wrap in a kitchen towel to keep the stack warm.

5. Place tempeh and peppers in warm tortillas and garnish with cilantro, avocado, and Easy Salsa Fresca.

>> SERVES 4 <<

1 tablespoon flour

1–2 teaspoons chili powder

1 teaspoon salt

1 teaspoon garlic powder

1 teaspoon minced onion

1 teaspoon ground cumin

¼ cup lime juice

1 tablespoon plus 2 teaspoons olive oil, divided

1 (8-ounce) package tempeh, cut into ¼" slices

1 medium onion, peeled and thinly sliced

1 medium red or green bell pepper, seeded and thinly sliced

4 (10") flour tortillas

¼ cup finely chopped cilantro

1 medium ripe avocado, sliced

1 recipe Easy Salsa Fresca (see Chapter 6)

BLACK BEAN and CHEESE EMPANADAS

» SERVES 4–6 «

- 1 tablespoon oil
- 1 cup finely chopped zucchini
- 1 small onion, peeled and minced
- 1 tablespoon tomato paste
- 1 teaspoon cumin
- 1 teaspoon salt
- ½ teaspoon black pepper
- 1 (15-ounce) can black beans, drained and rinsed
- ½ cup vegan mozzarella shreds
- 2½ cups flour
- 1 teaspoon baking powder
- 1 teaspoon salt
- ½ cup vegan nonhydrogenated vegetable shortening, chilled
- ½ cup ice water
- 1 tablespoon vinegar
- 1 recipe Avocado Sauce (see Chapter 6)

Ooooooh, empanadas! If you're a fan of Mexican food, you need to learn how to make these now. So please drop everything and start gathering the ingredients. Once you take your first rich, flaky, savory, cheesy bite, you'll know it was all worth it.

« – »

1. In a large sauté pan over medium-high heat, pour in olive oil and sauté zucchini and onions until onions are translucent, about 3–4 minutes. Then stir in tomato paste, cumin, salt, and pepper. Add black beans and stir, mashing beans slightly. Remove from heat. Stir in cheese. Set aside.

2. In a food processor, pulse together flour, baking powder, and salt.

3. Drop in shortening 1 tablespoon at a time. If doing by hand, use two knives or a pastry cutter. Pulse or mix by hand until mixture looks like coarse crumbs.

4. In a small bowl, mix ice water and vinegar. Add to dough mixture 1 tablespoon at a time, pulsing after each addition until a tablespoonful of dough holds together when pressed into a ball. Do not overmix.

5. Roll dough into a large ball, then divide into 16 balls. Cover and refrigerate at least 1 hour.

6. Preheat oven to 375°F. Line a baking sheet with parchment paper.

7. On a floured surface, roll each dough ball out to ⅛" thickness.

8. Spoon 2 tablespoons of bean mixture onto each dough round. Brush edge of dough with water and fold in half. Crimp edges shut by hand or with a fork, sealing in filling.

9. Bake 20 minutes or until golden brown. Serve with Avocado Sauce.

ORECCHIETTE *with* CREAM SAUCE *and* PEAS

Orecchia means "ear" in Italian. This pasta shape is a slightly toothsome little disk that holds sauce and peas in its little scoop perfectly.

« - »

1. In a large pot, add Orecchiette to salted boiling water and cook according to package directions. Drain and set aside.

2. In a large sauté pan over medium-low heat, cook onions and garlic with olive oil until onions are transparent, about 3–4 minutes. Add vegetable broth, peas, salt, and pepper and bring to a boil. Simmer until peas are tender but not mushy, about 5 minutes.

3. Reduce heat to low and add yeast, half & half, and Parmesan, and whisk gently until sauce is thick, about 4 minutes.

4. Pour sauce over pasta and serve.

>> SERVES 4 <<

- 1 (1-pound) package dry Orecchiette
- ¼ cup finely chopped onion
- 2 cloves garlic, chopped
- 2 tablespoons olive oil
- 2 cups vegetable broth
- 1 cup frozen petite peas
- 1 teaspoon salt
- ½ teaspoon black pepper
- 2 tablespoons nutritional yeast
- 1½ cups vegan half & half, unsweetened
- 2 tablespoons vegan Parmesan

LENTIL BOLOGNESE

Lily Allen and Rick Ross both feature Bolognese in their song lyrics—I know how they must feel, because this lentil variety is inspirational, comforting, and delicious.

« - »

1. Boil water to cook pasta, cooking until just al dente, drain.

2. In a large sauté pan over medium-high heat, add celery, onion, carrots, garlic, and olive oil and cook until onion is translucent, about 3–4 minutes. Pour in tomatoes and Chianti, cook until sauce has reduced by about ⅓, about 8 minutes. Season with thyme, salt, and pepper.

3. Stir almond milk into sauce and add lentils, stirring until heated through. Top with Parmesan and serve over pasta.

>> SERVES 4 <<

- 1 pound dry spaghetti
- ½ cup chopped celery
- ½ cup chopped onion
- ½ cup chopped carrots
- 2 cloves garlic, minced
- 2 tablespoons olive oil
- 1 (28-ounce) can crushed tomatoes
- 1 cup vegan Chianti
- ½ teaspoon dry thyme
- 1 teaspoon salt
- ½ teaspoon black pepper
- ½ cup almond milk
- 2 cups cooked brown lentils
- 2 tablespoons vegan Parmesan

SWEDISH MEATBALLS *with* GRAVY

2 (8-ounce) packages of tempeh

½ cup bread crumbs

1 cup finely chopped onion

½ teaspoon salt

½ teaspoon black pepper

¼ teaspoon allspice

¼ teaspoon ground nutmeg

4 tablespoons olive oil

¼ cup flour

4 cups vegetable broth

1 tablespoon vegan Worcestershire sauce

1 cup vegan half & half, unsweetened

2 tablespoons chopped Italian parsley

Tempeh does something fun when you steam it—it becomes a pliable substance just waiting to be formed into meatballs. These Swedish-inspired meatballs are lightly spiced and smothered in gravy.

1. Break up tempeh with your hands into small pieces and place in a steamer basket over boiling water. Cover tightly with a lid and steam 15 minutes.

2. Preheat oven to 350°F.

3. In a large bowl combine steamed tempeh, bread crumbs, onion, salt, pepper, allspice, and nutmeg. Using your hands, mix thoroughly. Shape into 1-ounce balls; a 1-ounce cookie dough scooper is perfect for this job. Place balls in a heated medium sauté pan in batches with a few tablespoons of olive oil and brown on all sides over medium-high heat. Set meatballs on a baking sheet and bake 10 minutes.

4. To the same pan add flour, whisking it into the oil. Cook flour until golden. While whisking, add vegetable broth and Worcestershire sauce to the pan. With the heat turned to low, slowly add half & half and simmer until gravy is lightly thick, about 5 minutes.

5. Pour gravy over baked meatballs in a serving dish and sprinkle with chopped parsley.

MUSHROOM STROGANOFF

Rich doesn't begin to describe the flavor profile of this hearty and filling pasta dish. It's perennially popular among my catering clients as well as my family. Serve with a generous basket of Ranch Garlic Bread (see Chapter 4) and sit back and accept the compliments to the chef.

« – »

1. In a 4-quart pot, bring 2 quarts water to a boil.

2. In a large sauté pan over medium-high heat, cook portobello mushrooms in small batches in a few teaspoons olive oil. Let mushrooms slightly brown and remove from pan; cook next batch adding oil a teaspoon at a time when needed. Set aside.

3. Add onions to the pan and cook until translucent and beginning to turn golden, about 5 minutes. Add button mushrooms to pan and salt. Use another teaspoon oil if the pan is too dry. Cook the mushrooms 10 minutes, stirring occasionally.

4. Put pasta in boiling water. Cook for time indicated on package while proceeding to the next step.

5. Add vegetable broth and cognac (if using) to the button mushrooms. Cook 10–15 minutes until liquid has reduced and can coat the back of a spoon.

6. Place pasta in a large serving dish. Toss with vegan butter and chopped parsley.

7. Lower the heat on the mushroom mixture and stir in Vegan Sour Cream. Bring just to a simmer and add portobello mushrooms back to pan, stirring to heat through.

8. Pour stroganoff over pasta and get busy eating.

» SERVES 4 «

1 pound portobello mushrooms, cut into ¼" slices

2 tablespoons olive oil

1 medium onion, peeled and chopped

1 (6-ounce) package button mushrooms, chopped

1 teaspoon salt

1 pound fettuccine, or pasta noodle of choice

1 cup vegetable broth

2 tablespoons cognac (optional)

1 tablespoon vegan butter, melted

1 tablespoon chopped fresh parsley

1 cup Vegan Sour Cream (see Chapter 6)

CORN DOGS *with* TANGY MUSTARD DIPPING SAUCE

Here's a vegan version of the carnival classic that you can make at home in a pinch. Need I say more?

» – «

1. Prepare deep fryer according to directions, or heat 4" of oil in a heavy pot to 375°F.

2. In a small bowl, combine soy milk and apple cider vinegar, then set aside.

3. In a medium bowl, stir together Bisquick, cornmeal, and seasoned salt.

4. Add soy milk-vinegar mixture and onion to dry ingredients and stir just until combined.

5. Pour batter into a drinking glass until it is about ¾ full.

6. Prepare hot dogs by placing a stick in each dog and rolling it in flour.

7. When oil is ready, dip each floured hot dog into the drinking glass full of batter.

8. Wearing an oven mitt, place battered hot dog into heated oil, holding the stick carefully, and cook 4–6 minutes or until very golden brown.

9. Serve with Tangy Mustard Sauce.

Oil (for frying)

1 cup soy milk

1 tablespoon apple cider vinegar

1 cup Bisquick Original Pancake and Baking Mix

½ cup cornmeal

1 teaspoon seasoned salt

¼ medium onion, peeled and grated

6 vegan hot dogs

6 Popsicle sticks or chopsticks

4 tablespoons flour

Tangy Mustard Sauce

In a small bowl, mix mustard, mayonnaise, agave, and vinegar with a whisk until very well combined.

½ cup Dijon mustard

¼ cup vegan mayonnaise

¼ cup agave

1 tablespoon apple cider vinegar

SAVORY TWICE-BAKED POTATOES

4 large baking potatoes, scrubbed

1 (8-ounce) container vegan cream cheese

1 cup Vegan Sour Cream (see Chapter 6)

3 tablespoons vegan butter

1 teaspoon salt

½ teaspoon black pepper

1 clove garlic, crushed

2 tablespoons finely chopped chives

½ cup nutritional yeast

1½ cups vegan Cheddar shreds, divided

2 tablespoons vegan bacon bits

2 teaspoons paprika

Better than French fries or potato skins, these spuds are baked and mixed with cream cheese, sour cream, butter, chives, cheese, and bacon, then baked again until the filling is molten and fluffy.

« – »

1. Preheat oven to 350°F.

2. With a fork, poke each potato 4 or 5 times to release steam as it cooks. Place in the oven directly on the middle rack. Bake 1 hour.

3. Remove potatoes from oven and, holding with an oven mitt, slice each in half. Set on counter to cool.

4. Line a baking sheet with parchment paper.

5. Scoop out baked potato flesh into a large bowl, leaving ¼" of flesh in each potato shell.

6. In a medium bowl with a whisk, cream together cream cheese, Vegan Sour Cream, and butter.

7. Spoon cream cheese mixture into the bowl with the potatoes, using a masher to incorporate well. Add salt, pepper, garlic, chives, nutritional yeast, 1 cup Cheddar shreds, and bacon bits.

8. Stuff each baked potato shell with heaping tablespoonfuls of filling. Place on prepared baking sheet.

9. Sprinkle remaining ½ cup Cheddar shreds and paprika on top.

10. Bake 20 minutes and eat while piping hot.

TORTILLA SOUP

This soup goes together fast and is perfect for a cold night when you feel like something spicy.

« - »

1. In a medium sauté pan over medium-high heat, heat the olive oil and sauté celery, onion, corn, garlic, and jalapeño. Cook until onion is translucent, about 5 minutes. Add salt, pepper, and cumin; stir until cumin becomes very fragrant, about 1 minute.

2. Add vegetable broth and tomatoes. Bring to a boil, turn heat down to medium, and simmer 10 minutes. Remove from heat and stir in lime juice.

3. Ladle soup into bowls, top with cilantro and avocado slices, and garnish with tortilla chips.

» SERVES 4 «

1 tablespoon olive oil

½ cup chopped celery

½ cup chopped onion

½ cup corn, fresh-cut from cob

1 clove garlic, chopped

1 medium jalapeño, seeded and chopped

1 teaspoon salt

½ teaspoon black pepper

2 teaspoons cumin

6 cups vegetable broth

2 medium tomatoes, seeded and chopped

3 tablespoons lime juice

¼ cup finely chopped cilantro

1 medium ripe avocado, sliced

Tortilla chips (for garnish)

ITALIAN SAUSAGE and PEPPERS with VODKA MARINARA

- 1 medium red bell pepper, seeded and sliced
- 1 medium green bell pepper, seeded and sliced
- 1 medium onion, peeled and sliced
- 1 tablespoon oil
- 1 (14-ounce) package vegan Italian sausage
- 1 (6-ounce) package button mushrooms, chopped
- ½ cup vodka
- 6 cups marinara

For a quick and dirty dinner with a spicy kick, this is your answer. Vegan sausage is widely available, so be sure to test out lots of varieties before arriving at your favorite.

« – »

1. In a large sauté pan over medium-high heat, sauté peppers and onions in 1 tablespoon oil. Cook until onions are translucent and tender, about 5 minutes. Remove from pan and set aside.

2. Add sausages to the same pan and cook until browned on all sides, adding oil if needed to prevent sticking. Remove from pan.

3. Add mushrooms to the pan and sauté until they begin to slightly brown, 5–7 minutes.

4. Pour vodka into pan and stir; cook about 1 minute.

5. Pour marinara over vodka and bring to a boil. Lower heat to medium and cook 10 minutes.

6. Add peppers, onions, and sausages back to pan and heat through, about 5 minutes.

BEER BRAT–STUFFED PORTOBELLO MUSHROOMS *with* STEAK FRIES

So satisfying and filling, these portobello mushrooms are jammed with a creamy, cheesy beer brat mixture and baked.

- 4 portobello mushrooms
- 1 (8-ounce) container vegan cream cheese, softened
- 2 tablespoons vegan butter, softened
- 2 cups bread crumbs
- ¼ cup walnuts, finely ground
- ¼ cup nutritional yeast
- 2 teaspoons parsley
- 1 teaspoon salt
- ½ teaspoon black pepper
- 2 Tofurky Original Sausage Beer Brats, cut into 1" pieces
- 1 medium onion, peeled and chopped
- 1 clove garlic, chopped
- 1 tablespoon olive oil

1. Preheat oven to 350°F. Line a baking sheet with parchment paper. (If making Steak Fries start cooking those first.)

2. Remove stems from portobello mushrooms, discard any tough parts, finely chop the remaining stem pieces, and set aside. Place whole mushrooms on prepared baking sheet. (Put the Steak Fries in oven while you do this.)

3. In a large bowl, mix cream cheese and butter until well combined, then add bread crumbs, walnuts, nutritional yeast, parsley, salt, and pepper.

4. In a medium sauté pan over medium-high heat, sauté beer brats, onion, chopped mushrooms, and garlic in olive oil until onions are translucent, about 6 minutes. Remove from heat.

5. Add beer brat mixture to cream cheese and mix to combine.

6. Spoon into whole mushrooms, dividing evenly.

7. Bake 25 minutes. Serve with Steak Fries.

Steak Fries

- 1 pound baking potatoes
- 2 tablespoons olive oil
- 1 teaspoon garlic salt
- 1 recipe Garlic Chive Dip (see Chapter 6)

1. Preheat oven to 350°F. Line a baking sheet with parchment paper.

2. Peel and cut potatoes into planks about ¼" thick.

3. In a large bowl, toss potatoes with olive oil and garlic salt, coating well.

4. Place in a single layer on prepared baking sheet. Bake 35–40 minutes.

5. Serve with Garlic Chive Dip.

MONGOLIAN BEEF

» SERVES 4 «

1 (8-ounce) package of seitan
   strips

4 tablespoons cornstarch

1 teaspoon oil

2 cloves garlic, crushed

½ teaspoon minced fresh
   ginger

½ teaspoon red pepper flakes

½ cup light soy sauce

¼ cup brown sugar

1 medium carrot, cut into
   long, thin noodle-like strips

1 tablespoon oil

1 green onion, chopped on the
   diagonal

Cows everywhere do a little dance when they see
a recipe like this, which features protein that's
kinder and gentler but still tastes like the real deal.
Gingery-garlicky goodness is the result of this
super-quick stir-fry. Serve this dish over the rice
of your choice.

« – »

1. In a shallow dish, dredge seitan strips in cornstarch and
set aside.

2. In a medium sauté pan over medium-high heat, heat oil,
then add garlic and ginger, cooking until very fragrant,
1–2 minutes. Add red pepper flakes. Pour in soy sauce and
whisk in sugar. Sauce will slightly thicken as it simmers, about
3 minutes. Remove from heat and transfer sauce to a medium
bowl. Wipe out pan.

3. In the same pan over high heat, sauté seitan strips and
carrots in 1 tablespoon oil until carrots are tender-crisp, about
5 minutes. Pour sauce back into pan and cook an additional
2 minutes, remove from heat, and stir in green onion.

NOODLES with TOFU and CASHEW STIR-FRY

If you wanted to start your own vegan Asian takeout, this would be a recipe to include under "House Specials." Take out your wok and give it a spin—you get all the classic noodle house flavors, and it stir-fries up in a snap!

» SERVES 4 «

1 (16-ounce) package firm tofu, drained and diced into 1" cubes

½ cup cornstarch

2 tablespoons oil

1 medium red chili pepper, sliced

2 cloves garlic, chopped

1 teaspoon grated ginger

1 cup cashews

1 cup snow peas, halved

¼ cup hoisin

¼ cup light soy sauce

2 tablespoons brown sugar

3 tablespoons seasoned rice vinegar

¼ cup water

6 ounces lo mein noodles, cooked and drained

1. In a medium bowl, toss tofu and cornstarch. Remove tofu, shaking off excess cornstarch.

2. In a large sauté pan (or wok) over medium-high heat, sauté tofu in oil until golden brown. Remove tofu from pan.

3. In the same pan, sauté red chili pepper, garlic, ginger, cashews, and snow peas until very fragrant, about 1 minute.

4. Add hoisin, light soy sauce, brown sugar, vinegar, and water, and stir to combine. Add tofu back to the pan and stir in noodles. Use tongs to mix noodles into sauce.

5. Remove from heat and serve. Don't forget the chopsticks!

TAKEOUT FRIED RICE

Fried rice is exactly the reason why you want to make enough rice to have leftovers.

» SERVES 4 «

1 tablespoon sesame seeds

2 tablespoons olive oil

1 cup peas (thawed, if frozen)

2 medium carrots, diced

¼ pound shiitake mushrooms, sliced

4 green onions, cut into 1" pieces

4 cups cooked brown rice, at room temperature

3 tablespoons soy sauce

1. In a large sauté pan over high heat, add sesame seeds to dry pan and stir constantly until seeds turn light golden brown, then remove from pan.

2. Add oil to pan. Sauté peas, carrots, mushrooms, green onions, and rice. Stir constantly while adding soy sauce. Cook about 5 minutes.

3. Transfer to a serving dish and stir in sesame seeds.

SPRING ROLLS

» SERVES 4–6 «

- 6 ounces savory baked tofu, cut into long, thin pieces
- 1 medium carrot, julienned or grated
- 1 cup cooked glass noodles
- ½ cup bean sprouts
- ¼ cup finely chopped cilantro
- ¼ cup chopped basil leaves
- ¼ teaspoon sesame oil
- 1 tablespoon hoisin
- 6 spring-roll rice papers

Raw or fried, these vegan goodies are an essential addition to any Asian feast. Unlike the takeout varieties, which are invariably limp, cold, and sad, these will remain fresh and/or warm-crispy. The Wasabi Soy Dipping Sauce and Spicy Peanut Sauce (both in Chapter 6) make them even more awesome.

« - »

1. In a medium bowl, mix tofu, carrot, noodles, bean sprouts, cilantro, and basil. Add sesame oil and hoisin, and toss to coat evenly.

2. Fill a shallow dish halfway with water. Place one rice paper in at a time, allowing it to soak in water about 6 seconds or just until pliable. Let water drip off.

3. Spoon 2 heaping tablespoonfuls of filling onto wrapper. Fold the bottom up about ¼ of the way over filling, fold in each side, and then continue rolling toward the top edge.

4. Serve spring rolls with Wasabi Soy Dipping Sauce (see Chapter 6).

Crispy Fried Spring Rolls

1. Prepare Spring Rolls as previously directed.

2. Heat about 3 inches of oil in a frying pan over medium-high heat. Heat oil to 375°F or until bubbles appear around a chopstick when inserted in oil.

3. Carefully place spring rolls in oil two at a time depending on the size of the pan. Fry on each side until golden brown, about 3–5 minutes.

4. Place on paper towels.

5. Serve with Spicy Peanut Sauce (see Chapter 6).

TAKEOUT ORANGE TOFU

For this Americanized variation of the classic sweet and sour, double the sauce because it keeps well in the fridge and tastes great over veggies and rice.

1. In a medium saucepan over medium-high heat, combine 1 cup water, orange zest, orange juice, lemon juice, vinegar, soy sauce, brown sugar, pepper flakes, ginger, and garlic. Bring to a boil, stirring occasionally.

2. In a small bowl, whisk together cornstarch and ½ cup water. Add to the saucepan. Bring back to a boil, then turn heat down to medium-low; cook until sauce has thickened, about 5 minutes. Remove from heat.

3. In a shallow dish, stir together flour, salt, and pepper, then add tofu and stir to coat all pieces in flour mixture.

4. In a large sauté pan over medium-high heat, add about 2 tablespoons of oil. Cook tofu in batches, frying until golden and very crispy on each side. Drain on paper towels.

5. Add tofu to sauce and stir in green onions. Serve immediately.

1½ cups water, divided

Zest of 1 medium orange

2 tablespoons orange juice

3 tablespoons lemon juice

½ cup rice wine vinegar

3 tablespoons light soy sauce

¾ cup brown sugar

¼ teaspoon red pepper flakes

½ teaspoon grated ginger

1 clove garlic, crushed

2 tablespoons cornstarch

½ cup flour

1 teaspoon salt

½ teaspoon black pepper

1 (16-ounce) package firm tofu, drained and cut into 1" pieces

Oil (for frying)

2 green onions, chopped on the diagonal

WONTON SAMOSAS

½ teaspoon cumin seeds

2 tablespoons oil plus more for frying wonton wrappers, divided

1 pound potatoes, peeled and chopped into ½" cubes

2 cloves garlic, minced

1 teaspoon salt

½ teaspoon turmeric

½ cup peas

⅓ cup water

¼ cup cilantro, finely chopped

1 package vegan wonton wrappers

2 teaspoons tamarind paste (optional)

1 recipe Spicy Peanut Sauce (see Chapter 6)

When you can't decide between Indian and Asian for dinner, look to this dish to satisfy your craving for fusion food. Of course, this is deep-fried, so it falls squarely in the category of fusion junk food, but that doesn't mean we love it any less. (In fact, it's just the opposite.)

« – »

1. In a medium sauté pan over medium-high heat, sauté cumin seeds in oil until fragrant, about 1 minute. Turn heat down to medium; add potatoes and garlic and cover. Cook about 10 minutes, stirring occasionally. Add salt, turmeric, peas, and water and stir. Cover and cook until water is absorbed and potatoes are tender, adding more water a few tablespoons at a time if necessary to cook potatoes. Remove from heat and stir in cilantro.

2. Heat about 3" oil in a deep, medium sauté pan to 360°F.

3. On each wonton wrapper, wet edges with water, place a heaping teaspoonful of filling in the middle, and fold into a triangle, sealing in filling by crimping edges with a fork.

4. Fry each wonton in oil about 2–3 minutes, turning until each side is golden brown. Drain on paper towels.

5. If using, stir tamarind paste into the Spicy Peanut Sauce. Serve alongside the fried wontons.

TOFU EGGPLANT TIKKA MASALA

We don't need no stinking yogurt, especially when there's soygurt! And with that, we can create the creamy Indian classic that is tikka masala. If you're looking for a meatier rendition, sub out the tofu with a vegan meat product.

« – »

1. In a large bowl, whisk yogurt, tikka masala spice blend, ginger, garlic, and salt.

2. Cut tofu and eggplant into 1" dices. Add to yogurt marinade and let sit at least 1 hour on the counter.

3. In a large sauté pan over medium heat, sauté onion in olive oil until translucent, about 5 minutes. Add tomatoes to the pan and cook until they begin to break down, about 4 minutes.

4. Add marinated tofu and eggplant with yogurt marinade to the sauté pan. Cook until eggplant is tender, being careful not to break up tofu too much, about 10 minutes.

5. Stir in peas and heat through. Taste to see if it needs more tikka masala spice. Add 1 teaspoon at a time to desired heat. Remove from heat.

6. Stir in cilantro and lemon juice and serve.

» SERVES 4 «

- 1 cup unsweetened vegan yogurt
- 3 teaspoons tikka masala spice blend
- 1 teaspoon grated ginger
- 1 clove garlic, chopped
- 1 teaspoon salt
- 1 (16-ounce) package extra-firm tofu, drained
- 1 large eggplant
- 1 medium onion, peeled and diced
- 1 tablespoon olive oil
- 1 medium tomato, seeded and diced
- 1 cup frozen peas
- 1 tablespoon finely chopped cilantro
- 1 tablespoon lemon juice

• CHAPTER 4 •

Crusts and Carbs

• Pizza Pies and Badass Breads •

BASIC PIZZA DOUGH

You can find vegan pizza dough at your favorite grocery that stocks products that are kind to animals and the planet, but if time allows, give this homemade dough a whirl. It's easy enough and awfully tasty.

-- -------------------------------------- --

1. In a small bowl, mix water and yeast.

2. In a large bowl, mix flour and salt, make a well in the center, and pour in water-yeast mixture and olive oil.

3. Mix with a wooden spoon or dough hook in a mixer until mixture forms a ball.

4. Turn out onto a floured board and knead 5 minutes. Transfer to a greased medium bowl and let dough rise in a warm place for 90 minutes.

5. Divide dough into number of pizzas desired. Place dough on a floured surface and roll dough out to desired size or shape by hand. Place dough on a baking sheet liberally coated with cornmeal or on a pizza pan.

6. Add desired toppings and bake at 425°F for 20–25 minutes.

>> MAKES 1 (16"), 2 (12"), OR 4 (8") PIZZAS <<

1 cup warm water*

1 package active dry yeast

3 cups flour

1 teaspoon salt

3 tablespoons olive oil

*When poured across wrist, the water should feel slightly warmer than body temperature.

SUPER-EASY PIZZA SAUCE

There's nothing like fresh marinara. Do yourself a favor and make a few batches to have on hand for when a pizza craving strikes.

-- -------------------------------------- --

In a large bowl, mix all the ingredients together and allow to sit at least 1 hour before using to allow flavors to marry. You will need roughly ½ cup sauce per 12" pizza. Leftover sauce is also great on pasta.

>> MAKES 2½ CUPS <<

2 cups crushed tomatoes

1 (6-ounce) can tomato paste

¼ cup nutritional yeast

2 tablespoons sugar

1 teaspoon dried basil, or 1 table-spoon fresh, chopped fine

1 teaspoon dried oregano, or 2 teaspoons fresh, chopped fine

¼ teaspoon marjoram

¼ teaspoon black pepper

1–2 cloves garlic, crushed

TANDOORI TEMPEH PIZZA on ONION-GARLIC NAAN with CUCUMBER YOGURT SAUCE

1 (6-ounce) carton plain unsweetened vegan yogurt

2 tablespoons lemon juice

2 cloves garlic, minced

1 teaspoon grated fresh ginger

1 teaspoon salt

1 teaspoon cumin

1 teaspoon coriander

1 teaspoon chili powder (optional)

½ teaspoon paprika

½ teaspoon turmeric

1 (8-ounce) package tempeh, chopped into 2" cubes

½ recipe Onion-Garlic Naan (see recipe in this chapter), or 6 whole-wheat pitas

¼ medium onion, peeled and sliced thin

2 tablespoons olive oil

1 (6-ounce) carton plain un-sweetened vegan yogurt

1 medium cucumber, peeled, seeded, and finely chopped or grated

1 tablespoon lemon juice

2 teaspoons chopped fresh mint leaves

½ teaspoon sugar

½ teaspoon salt

This super-flavorful pizza with an Indian flair features warming spices and a cool cucumber dip. It reminds me of something you could order at a small out-of-the-way Indian eatery in London...best enjoyed at 2 a.m. after consuming many pints.

« – »

1. In a large shallow dish, add yogurt, lemon juice, garlic, ginger, salt, cumin, coriander, chili powder, paprika, and turmeric, using a whisk to combine. Add tempeh and marinate overnight in the refrigerator for best results.

2. Preheat oven to 500°F. Line a cookie sheet with parchment paper.

3. Place cooked naan on cookie sheet. Top with marinated tempeh and onions. Drizzle with olive oil.

4. Place cookie sheet under the broiler and broil 4–6 minutes, watching carefully. Tempeh and onions should brown, and naan should crisp but not burn.

5. Serve with Cucumber Yogurt Sauce.

Cucumber Yogurt Sauce

1. In a medium bowl, mix together yogurt, cucumber, lemon juice, mint, sugar, and salt.

2. Keep refrigerated; use within 3 days.

BAKED ZITI PIZZA

If you thought pasta alone was a filling meal, try topping a pizza with it! You don't need to be running a marathon to enjoy this ultimate carb-load treat featuring three kinds of cheese and a delectable crusty texture.

« - »

1. Preheat oven to 475°F. Place rolled or stretched Basic Pizza Dough on a prepared 16" pizza pan or a greased and cornmeal-sprinkled cookie sheet.

2. Spread ½ cup Super-Easy Pizza Sauce on dough evenly. Top with tablespoonfuls of Vegan Ricotta, spreading out into a thin layer over sauce.

3. In a large bowl, toss together ziti, 1 cup Super-Easy Pizza Sauce, 1 tablespoon oil, and ½ cup cheese shreds.

4. In a small bowl, mix ground walnuts, 1 teaspoon oil, nutritional yeast, and salt (this will be the Parmesan).

5. Pour ziti mixture on crust topped with sauce and ricotta. Top with Parmesan mixture and remaining cheese shreds. Cut a piece of foil to cover ziti, leaving edges of crust uncovered.

6. Bake 20–25 minutes, removing foil the last 5 minutes of the cooking time.

» SERVES 4 «

- **1 recipe of Basic Pizza Dough, uncooked (see recipe in this chapter)**
- **1½ cups Super-Easy Pizza Sauce (see recipe in this chapter), divided**
- **1 cup Vegan Ricotta (see Chapter 6)**
- **3 cups cooked ziti pasta**
- **1 tablespoon plus 1 teaspoon oil, divided**
- **1½ cups vegan mozzarella shreds**
- **½ cup walnuts, ground**
- **¼ cup nutritional yeast**
- **Pinch salt**

MEATBALL PIZZA
with PEPPERS *and* ONIONS

1 recipe Basic Pizza Dough, uncooked (see recipe in this chapter)

1 medium onion, peeled and thinly sliced

2 medium bell peppers, seeded and thinly sliced

2 teaspoons olive oil

1 teaspoon salt

1 clove garlic, chopped

¾ cup Super-Easy Pizza Sauce (see recipe in this chapter)

1 recipe Meatballs (see Meatball Subwich in Chapter 2), or 1 (12-ounce) package frozen vegan meatballs

1 cup vegan mozzarella shreds

Don't like bell peppers? Add more onions. Not an onion fan? Add more meatballs. Don't like sauce? Well, I can't help you there, but you get the idea. You can make pizza recipes your own by ramping up the toppings that speak to your deepest foodie desires.

1. Preheat oven to 475°F. Place rolled or stretched dough on a prepared 16" pizza pan or a greased and cornmeal-sprinkled cookie sheet.

2. In a large sauté pan over medium-high heat, cook onions and peppers in olive oil until tender, about 6 minutes. Add salt and garlic, cook 1 more minute.

3. Pour pizza sauce over dough and spread evenly, followed with meatballs, peppers, and onions. Top with cheese.

4. Bake 20–25 minutes. Slice and enjoy!

SPICY ONION *and* SAUSAGE PIZZA

» SERVES 4 «

- 1 recipe of Basic Pizza Dough, uncooked (see recipe in this chapter)
- 1 (14-ounce) tube Lightlife Gimme Lean Sausage, pulled apart into 1" chunks
- 1–2 teaspoons dried crushed red chili flakes, depending on how spicy you want it
- 2 teaspoons olive oil
- ¾ cup Super-Easy Pizza Sauce (see recipe in this chapter)
- 1 medium onion, peeled and sliced thin
- 1 cup vegan mozzarella shreds

Make like you are in Little Italy and serve this up to your omnivorous friends. For the finale, let them know what they just ate was pig friendly and see the look of shock when it dawns on them they just ate a vegan sausage pizza. Then expect a few converts.

1. Preheat oven to 475°F. Place rolled or stretched dough on a prepared 16" pizza pan or a greased and cornmeal-sprinkled cookie sheet.

2. In a large sauté pan over medium-high heat, cook sausage chunks and red chili flakes in olive oil until browned on all sides. Remove from heat.

3. Pour pizza sauce over dough and spread evenly, followed with sausage and onions. Top with cheese.

4. Bake for 20–25 minutes.

DEEP-DISH HAWAIIAN PIZZA

» SERVES 4–6 «

- 1 recipe Basic Pizza Dough, uncooked (see recipe in this chapter)
- 2 cups Super-Easy Pizza Sauce (see recipe in this chapter)
- 1 (5-ounce) package vegan deli slices, such as Tofurky Deli Slices Hickory Smoked, chopped
- 1 (15-ounce) can pineapple chunks, drained
- 2 cups vegan mozzarella shreds

So good and so junky! Whoever thought to pair salty meat with pineapple was clearly a genius. This vegan rendition features lots and lots of deli slices, canned fruit, and mozzarella shreds married in a deep, delicious crust.

1. Preheat oven to 475°F. Press dough into bottom and sides of a greased and cornmeal-sprinkled 12" springform pan.

2. Pour Super-Easy Pizza Sauce over dough followed by chopped deli slices, pineapple, and mozzarella shreds.

3. Bake 40–45 minutes or until crust is golden brown and cheese is melted. Let cool about 10 minutes before cutting. (Good luck eating without a fork!)

EGGPLANT PARMESAN PIZZA

Deep-fried eggplant Parmesan is a delicious dish that has found its spiritual home on top of a pizza. Load on the cheese and take this hybrid for a spin. This pizza keeps really well, so look forward to leftovers for breakfast.

1 recipe **Basic Pizza Dough**, uncooked (see recipe in this chapter)

1 cup **Super-Easy Pizza Sauce** (see recipe in this chapter)

½ cup **walnuts, ground**

¼ cup **nutritional yeast**

1 teaspoon **oil**

Pinch **salt**

1 cup **nondairy milk**

1 cup **flour**

1 cup **bread crumbs**

½ teaspoon **dried oregano**

½ teaspoon **dried basil**

1 teaspoon **salt**

Olive oil (for frying)

1 medium **eggplant, thinly sliced**

2 cups **vegan mozzarella shreds**

1. Preheat oven to 475°F. Shape dough on a 16" pizza pan or on a greased and cornmeal-sprinkled cookie sheet.

2. Spread pizza sauce evenly over dough.

3. In a small bowl, mix ground walnuts, nutritional yeast, oil, and pinch salt (this will be the Parmesan).

4. In three separate shallow dishes, place milk, flour, and bread crumbs. Add the oregano and basil to the bread crumbs, and add 1 teaspoon salt to the flour.

5. In a large sauté pan, heat about 2 teaspoons olive oil over medium heat.

6. Dip each eggplant slice into milk, dredge in flour, and dip in milk again, then lastly dip in bread crumbs.

7. Fry eggplant in heated oil about 3 minutes on each side until golden brown; transfer to paper-lined plate.

8. Once all the eggplant is cooked, place in a spiral pattern on the pizza sauce and top with mozzarella cheese and Parmesan.

9. Bake 20–25 minutes. Slice and enjoy!

THAI PIZZA

» SERVES 4 «

1 recipe Basic Pizza Dough, uncooked (see recipe in this chapter)

1 teaspoon tamarind paste

1 red chili pepper, diced (optional)

1 recipe Spicy Peanut Sauce (see Chapter 6)

2 (8-ounce) packages tempeh

1 medium carrot, cut into long, thin strands or grated

2 green onions, cut into long, thin strands

3 tablespoons crushed peanuts

½ cup bean sprouts

¼ cup finely chopped cilantro

Who would think to use peanut sauce in place of pizza sauce? East meets West in this truly unique pie that melds savory, spicy, and fresh flavors with crunchy, creamy, and meaty textures.

« – »

1. Preheat oven to 475°F. Shape dough on a 16" pizza pan or on a cornmeal-sprinkled cookie sheet.

2. In a small bowl, mix tamarind paste and chili (if using) into Spicy Peanut Sauce. Cut tempeh into 1" cubes. In a separate small bowl, mix tempeh and half of Spicy Peanut Sauce, coating all pieces.

3. Spread the other half of Spicy Peanut Sauce evenly on the dough. Top with marinated tempeh and any remaining sauce.

4. Arrange carrot and green onion over tempeh.

5. Bake 20–25 minutes.

6. Top with peanuts, bean sprouts, and cilantro.

BLACK BEAN TACO PIZZA

Anything with refried beans in it automatically moves to the head of the pack when it comes to junk food. This totally cravable pizza features a mix of pizza sauce and the aforementioned beans—it's like a flat taco!

« – »

1. Preheat oven to 475°F. Shape dough on a 16" pizza pan or on a greased and cornmeal-sprinkled cookie sheet.

2. In a small bowl, mix black beans and tomato sauce, and spread on pizza dough.

3. In a 10" skillet over medium-high heat, sauté tempeh in oil until golden brown, about 5 minutes. Stir in flour, chili powder, salt, garlic powder, cumin, and minced onion, and cook until spices become fragrant and tempeh is coated in spice mixture. Add water to pan and stir well. Cook 1 minute.

4. Spread tempeh mixture over black beans.

5. Bake 20 minutes.

6. Slice with a pizza cutter into slices. Top each slice with lettuce, tomatoes, avocado, cilantro, onion, and a dollop of Creamy Southwestern Dip.

» SERVES 4 «

1 recipe Basic Pizza Dough, uncooked (see recipe in this chapter)

1 (15-ounce) can refried black beans

½ cup tomato sauce

1 (8-ounce) package tempeh, crumbled

1 tablespoon oil

1 tablespoon flour

1–2 teaspoons chili powder

1 teaspoon salt

1 teaspoon garlic powder

1 teaspoon cumin

1 teaspoon minced onion

½ cup water

4 cups lettuce leaves

1 medium tomato, chopped

1 medium ripe avocado, chopped

¼ cup chopped cilantro

¼ medium onion, peeled and chopped

1 recipe Creamy Southwestern Dip (see Chapter 6)

PESTO CHICKEN PIZZA
with CREAMY GARLIC SAUCE

1 recipe Basic Pizza Dough, uncooked (see recipe in this chapter)

1 (9-ounce) package vegan chicken strips such as Beyond Meat Beyond Chicken Strips

1 recipe Basil Pesto (see Chapter 6)

3 cloves garlic, chopped

2 tablespoons olive oil

4 tablespoons flour

1¼ cups nondairy milk

½ cup vegetable broth

1 (15-ounce) can white beans, drained and puréed well with ½ cup vegetable broth

½ cup nutritional yeast

1 teaspoon salt

½ teaspoon black pepper

This white pizza flies in the face of conventional pies and comes together in a pinch. Plus, it features Beyond Meat, a major star in the world of vegan junk food.

« – »

1. Preheat oven to 475°F. Shape dough on a 16" pizza pan or on a greased and cornmeal-sprinkled cookie sheet.

2. Cut chicken strips into thin strips. In a medium bowl, add pesto (save a few tablespoons for drizzling on pizza) and chicken strips, stirring to coat chicken pieces. Set aside.

3. In a large skillet over medium heat, sauté garlic in olive oil until it becomes very fragrant, being careful not to let it brown. Add flour to the pan and mix with a whisk, stirring flour into oil. Cook 1 minute.

4. Slowly add milk, stirring constantly. Stir in bean mixture, nutritional yeast, salt, and pepper, cooking until sauce is creamy and thick. Add more milk a few tablespoons at a time if sauce becomes too thick. Remove from heat.

5. Spread sauce over pizza. Top with chicken strips. Drizzle a few tablespoons of Basil Pesto over pizza.

6. Bake 20–25 minutes, slice, and gobble up.

ROSEMARY-GARLIC POTATO PIZZA

Truth be told; this is a bit more gourmet than the other junk food offerings in this book. But it's still not something that would be on Weight Watchers' list of approved foods, so I think we're in the clear. This pizza boasts tender potatoes artfully layered over a creamy white garlic sauce with hints of rosemary. Can you say *divine*?

1. Preheat oven to 475°F. Shape dough on a 16" pizza pan or on a greased and cornmeal-sprinkled cookie sheet.

2. In a 4-quart saucepan over high heat, bring 2 quarts of water to a boil. Place potatoes in water and bring back to a boil. Cook 5–8 minutes, checking frequently. Potatoes should be al dente, softened but with a bite to them. Drain.

3. In a medium bowl, toss potatoes with olive oil, salt, and rosemary. Set aside.

4. Purée beans with broth until smooth, set aside.

5. In a large skillet over medium heat, sauté garlic in olive oil until it becomes very fragrant, being careful not to let it brown. Add flour to the pan and mix with a whisk, stirring flour into oil. Cook 1 minute.

6. Slowly add milk and bean mixture, stirring constantly. Stir in nutritional yeast, salt, and pepper, cooking until sauce is creamy and thick. Add more milk a few tablespoons at a time if sauce gets too thick. Remove from heat.

7. Spread sauce over pizza. Top with potatoes in a spiral pattern and drizzle with a small amount of olive oil.

8. Bake 20–25 minutes. Cool slightly, then cut and share.

VEGGIE CHEESE BAGUETTE PIZZA

» SERVES 4 «

2 cups sliced mushrooms

1 medium onion, peeled and thinly sliced

2 medium bell peppers, red or green, seeded and thinly sliced

2 tablespoons olive oil

1 clove garlic, minced

1 French bread baguette, cut in half lengthwise

1 cup Super-Easy Pizza Sauce (see recipe in this chapter)

2 cups vegan mozzarella shreds

Here's a dorm-room favorite revamped with vegan cheese. It's even easier to put together when you have your own kitchen, but it still tastes as mouthwateringly good as it did when you were studying for finals.

1. Preheat oven to 400°F. Line a baking sheet with foil.

2. In a medium skillet over medium heat, sauté mushrooms, onion, and peppers in olive oil until tender-crisp; add garlic and sauté 2 more minutes.

3. Place baguette halves on cookie sheet. Spread Super-Easy Pizza Sauce over each, followed by 1 cup cheese.

4. Divide mushroom mixture between baguette halves. Top with remaining cheese.

5. Bake 15 minutes or until cheese is melted and bread is crispy.

BARBECUED TEMPEH PIZZA

» SERVES 4 «

1 recipe Basic Pizza Dough, uncooked (see recipe in this chapter)

2 (8-ounce) packages tempeh

2 cups barbecue sauce

½ cup vegan mozzarella shreds

1 medium red onion, peeled and sliced thin

¼ cup finely chopped cilantro

½ cup Creamy Ranch Dressing (see Chapter 6)

Just a few key ingredients make this pizza really special: barbecued marinated tempeh, red onions, and cilantro. It's perfect for dipping into ranch dressing.

1. Preheat oven to 475°F. Shape dough on a 16" pizza pan or on a greased and cornmeal-sprinkled cookie sheet.

2. Slice tempeh into ¼" slices. Put half the barbecue sauce in a shallow dish and add sliced tempeh, turning to coat.

3. Spread the other half of the barbecue sauce on crust. Top with tempeh, cheese, and onions.

4. Bake 20 minutes.

5. Top with cilantro, drizzle with Creamy Ranch Dressing, slice, and devour.

ARTICHOKE *and* CARAMELIZED-ONION PIZZA *with* BALSAMIC REDUCTION

Sweet caramelized onions, tangy artichokes, and a rich Balsamic Reduction on a crisp, light crust. You could pay upward of $20 at the fancy new wood-fired pizza joint downtown for a similar pie, or you could build it at home for half the cost in less than 1 hour. Your pick.

« – »

1. Preheat oven to 475°F. Place rolled or stretched dough on a prepared 16" pizza pan or a greased and cornmeal-sprinkled cookie sheet.

2. In a medium sauté pan over medium-high heat, sauté onions in olive oil, stirring occasionally, allowing onions to cook down and turn a deep golden brown, about 10 minutes. Turn heat down and add salt and garlic. If the onions start to brown too much, lower heat; add a teaspoon of oil if they start to stick. Cook another 8–10 minutes, stirring occasionally. Remove from heat.

3. Spoon onions onto dough and spread evenly. Top with artichokes and cheese.

4. Bake 20–25 minutes.

5. Drizzle with Balsamic Reduction and enjoy while piping hot.

» SERVES 4 «

- **1 recipe of Basic Pizza Dough, uncooked (see recipe in this chapter)**
- **3 medium onions, peeled and thinly sliced**
- **1 tablespoon olive oil**
- **1 teaspoon salt**
- **1 clove garlic, chopped**
- **1 (14-ounce) can whole artichoke hearts, drained and quartered**
- **1 cup vegan mozzarella shreds**
- **1 recipe Balsamic Reduction (see Chapter 6)**

PIZZA DOUGH GARLIC ROLLS

» SERVES 6 «

1 recipe Basic Pizza Dough, uncooked (see recipe in this chapter)

1 cup vegan mozzarella shreds

3 cloves garlic, minced

1 teaspoon salt

½ teaspoon garlic powder

½ teaspoon dried basil

1 tablespoon chopped fresh parsley

¼ cup nutritional yeast

3 tablespoons olive oil

Sometimes the sauce and toppings just get in the way, right? The melted garlic cheese interior in these bad boys is to die for. You'll want to double the recipe if you have hungry teens to feed. These are delicious served with some Basil Pesto (see Chapter 6) for dipping.

1. Preheat oven to 350°F. Line a baking sheet with parchment paper.

2. Divide dough into 16–18 pieces. Roll pieces into balls.

3. In a small bowl, mix together cheese and garlic.

4. In each dough ball, press about a tablespoonful of cheese-garlic mixture into the center and close dough around it. Roll back into a smooth ball. Place on prepared baking sheet. Repeat for rest of dough balls.

5. Bake 20 minutes or until golden brown, shaking baking sheet halfway through cooking to help brown evenly.

6. In a large bowl, mix together salt, garlic powder, basil, parsley, and nutritional yeast.

7. When rolls are hot out of the oven, drizzle with olive oil, turning to coat.

8. Place oiled rolls a few at a time into nutritional yeast mixture, tossing to coat. Serve hot.

BEER CHEESE BREAD

» MAKES 1
(9" × 5") LOAF «

3 cups self-rising flour*

¼ cup brown sugar

1 (12-ounce) can vegan beer,
light-colored

⅓ cup vegan butter, melted

¼ cup nutritional yeast

1 recipe Green Chili Dip (see
Chapter 6)

*NOTE: If you do not have
self-rising flour, sift together
3 cups all-purpose flour, 4½
teaspoons baking powder, and
1 teaspoon salt.

Thankfully, several brewers make vegan-friendly beers. And despite the fact that it's a beverage, beer is an honorary junk food. With just a few ingredients, you have homemade bread that tastes slightly malty from the brew and super buttery. For a spicy Beer Cheese Bread, add ¼ cup chopped canned jalapeños to this recipe.

« – »

1. Preheat oven to 375°F. Lightly grease a 9" × 5" loaf pan.

2. In a medium bowl, mix flour and brown sugar. Add beer and mix just until dough is combined; do not overmix.

3. Spoon dough into prepared pan.

4. In a small bowl, mix butter and nutritional yeast and pour over dough.

5. Bake 40–50 minutes or until a knife comes out clean. Cool on a wire rack.

6. Serve with Green Chili Dip.

DROP BISCUITS

» MAKES 12
BISCUITS «

1¾ cups self-rising flour*

¾ cup nondairy milk

3 tablespoons vegan
mayonnaise

*NOTE: If you do not have
self-rising flour, sift together
3 cups all-purpose flour, 4½
teaspoons baking powder, and
1 teaspoon salt.

When you need a biscuit quick, look to this easy-peasy recipe. These beauties beg to be drowned in gravy or topped with butter and jam.

« – »

1. Preheat oven to 450°F. Lightly grease a cookie sheet.

2. In a medium bowl, mix flour, milk, and mayonnaise until just combined; do not overmix.

3. Drop by the heaping tablespoonful onto prepared baking sheet.

4. Bake 7–9 minutes or until tops begin to turn golden brown.

YEASTED DINNER ROLLS

Yeast rolls seem like a daunting undertaking, but they are a snap to make, and you can ignore them completely while they rise.

1 tablespoon vegan butter

1 tablespoon sugar

1 cup plus 2 tablespoons water, heated to 100°F

3 teaspoons active yeast

2 tablespoons ground flaxseeds

1 teaspoon salt

2½ cups flour

1. Preheat oven to 450°F. Grease a baking sheet.

2. In a large bowl, mix butter, sugar, water, and yeast until yeast dissolves. With your hands, mix in flaxseeds, salt, and flour until a smooth dough forms. Cover and let rise 1 hour.

3. Form dough into 8 balls and place on greased baking sheet 2" apart. Allow to rise a second time until doubled, about 30 minutes to 1 hour.

4. Bake 10–12 minutes or until golden brown.

RANCH GARLIC BREAD

I make this bread at catering events all the time, and people always want to know the mystery behind it. But there's really nothing to it! It's half herb and half garlic, which makes it a good side to a salad or soup.

½ cup vegan butter, softened

2 tablespoons dry Creamy Ranch Dressing mix (see Chapter 6)

2 cloves garlic, crushed

1 French bread baguette

1. Preheat oven to 375°F. Line a baking sheet with parchment paper.

2. In a small bowl, mix butter, dry Creamy Ranch Dressing mix, and garlic.

3. Slice baguette lengthwise or into 2" slices. Divide garlic mixture between two loaves or slices.

4. Place on prepared baking sheet and bake 10–15 minutes or until bread is toasted and golden. Best enjoyed warm.

GARLIC-ONION-CHEESE BREAD LOAF

**» MAKES 1
(9" × 5") LOAF «**

¾ cup soy milk

1 teaspoon apple cider vinegar

½ medium red onion, peeled
and chopped

3 cloves garlic, chopped

1 tablespoon plus 2 teaspoons
olive oil, divided

½ teaspoon black pepper

2 cups flour

2 teaspoons baking powder

1 teaspoon baking soda

1 teaspoon dried chives

1 teaspoon salt

1½ cups vegan Cheddar
shreds

This savory loaf benefits from a buttermilk-like flavor that comes when you mix soy milk and apple cider vinegar. Add vegan cheese to the mix for a truly memorable bread that only gets better when toasted and slathered with vegan butter.

1. Preheat oven to 400°F. Grease a 9" × 5" loaf pan.

2. In a small bowl, mix soy milk and apple cider vinegar; set aside.

3. In a medium sauté pan over medium-high heat, cook onion and garlic in 2 teaspoons olive oil, stirring constantly until onions are golden, about 8 minutes. Add pepper. Remove from heat.

4. In a medium bowl, mix flour, baking powder, baking soda, chives, and salt. Stir in soy milk-vinegar mixture, cheese, and onion-garlic mixture, mixing until just combined; do not overmix.

5. Pour mixture into prepared pan. Drizzle with 1 tablespoon olive oil.

6. Bake 25–30 minutes. Cool completely before cutting.

TEX-MEX CORN BREAD

There's corn bread and then there's corn bread. Anything but dry, anything but boring, this colorful and spicy twist on ordinary corn bread is the perfect vehicle for melting a generous smear of vegan butter. Savory eats in this baking dish, I tell ya.

» MAKES 6–8 SERVINGS «

1½ cups soy milk

1 tablespoon apple cider vinegar

1½ cups flour

1 cup cornmeal

2 teaspoons baking powder

2 tablespoons sugar

1 teaspoon salt

1 small onion, peeled and minced

1 clove garlic, minced

1 medium jalapeño pepper, seeded and chopped

1 medium red bell pepper, seeded and finely chopped

¼ cup vegan nonhydrogenated vegetable shortening, softened

2 tablespoons vegan butter, softened

1. Preheat oven to 350°F. Grease a 9" × 9" baking dish.

2. In a large bowl, mix soy milk and apple cider vinegar; set aside to thicken.

3. In a medium bowl, whisk together flour, cornmeal, baking powder, sugar, and salt.

4. To soy milk-vinegar mixture, add onion, garlic, jalapeño and red bell peppers, shortening, and butter.

5. Add flour ingredients to soy milk mixture and stir just to combine; do not overmix.

6. Pour into prepared baking dish.

7. Bake 40–45 minutes or until a toothpick comes out clean and top is golden brown.

PRETZEL ROLLS *or* BITES

Pretzel rolls make most every veggie burger extra special. With their soft and salty character, they are also great next to a bowl of soup or even a salad. For rolls big enough to handle a Beet Burger (see Chapter 2), make 8 rolls instead of 12.

» MAKES 12 ROLLS «

3 cups all-purpose flour

3 teaspoons active dry yeast

1 tablespoon plus 1 teaspoon salt

1 teaspoon sugar

1 cup water, heated to 100°F

¼ cup baking soda

1 tablespoon coarse salt

1. To a mixer bowl fitted with a dough hook, add flour, yeast, 1 teaspoon salt, and sugar. With mixer running on low, add the warm water slowly until a smooth dough forms. Mix 5 minutes. Alternatively, knead by hand 10 minutes.

2. Place dough in a large lightly oiled bowl, cover with a towel, and leave in a warm place to rise until it has doubled; about 30 minutes to 1 hour.

3. Once dough has doubled, punch it down and evenly divide it into 12 balls. For pretzel bites, divide into 6 balls, rolling each into a long coil. With a sharp knife, cut each coil into 10 pieces. Place balls or bites on a baking sheet and allow to rise 30 minutes.

4. While dough is rising, preheat oven to 450°F and bring 4 quarts water, baking soda, and 1 tablespoon salt to a boil. Turn down to a slow boil. In small batches to prevent sticking, add dough balls carefully to the water and let boil 1 minute, turning each halfway through. Remove dough from the water with a slotted spoon and return to the baking sheet.

5. When dough balls are all boiled, slash an X into the top of each with a lame or scissors. (Slashes aren't needed if you're making pretzel bites.) Sprinkle with coarse salt. Bake 15 minutes or until deeply browned.

6. Cool completely on a wire rack.

ONION-GARLIC NAAN

» MAKES 12 NAAN «

1 large onion, peeled and finely chopped

1 tablespoon olive oil

2 cloves garlic, chopped

¾ cup lukewarm water

⅓ cup vegan butter, melted

1 teaspoon salt

3–3¼ cups flour

Most naan you find at the market or out at restaurants is made with buttermilk, an ingredient that's verboten for vegans. It's not a problem here, as I've found a way to create the same light texture while bypassing animal products altogether. Use this as a base for a pizza, to dip in hummus, or to munch on its own. Either way, it satisfies a bread craving.

1. In a medium sauté pan over high heat, cook onion in the olive oil, stirring occasionally about 4 minutes. Add garlic. When onions are translucent and just golden brown, remove from heat.

2. In a large bowl using a wooden spoon, combine onion-garlic mixture, water, melted butter, and salt. Begin adding 3 cups of flour ½ cup at a time. Add the extra ¼ cup flour only if you need it to form a smooth dough that doesn't stick to your hands.

3. Form dough into a large ball and cut into 16 equal pieces; roll each piece into a ball. On a lightly floured surface, roll each ball into an 8" circle.

4. In a large dry skillet over medium-high heat, place each naan in the pan, about 3–4 minutes on each side.

CHAPTER 5

Festive Grub

• Vegan Party Essentials •

OVEN-ROASTED CORN *with*
CHEESY CAYENNE LIME BUTTER

» SERVES 6 «

6 ears of corn

6 tablespoons vegan butter, melted

Juice of 3 medium limes

2 teaspoons salt

½ teaspoon cayenne pepper

¼ cup nutritional yeast

These ears give regular old corn on the cob a serious run for its money. The hardest part of this recipe is shucking the corn, so why not bring this to your next barbecue? You're sure to make a boatload of new friends—and quite possibly some new fans.

1. If making in the oven: preheat oven to 400°F.

2. In a large baking dish, place corn, butter, lime juice, salt, cayenne pepper, and nutritional yeast. Roll corn around in mixture. Cover tightly with foil.

3. Bake 35 minutes.

4. If making on the grill: peel back husk and remove silk; replace husk and grill about 30 minutes or until tender.

5. To serve, remove husk and place corn on a serving platter; brush each ear with melted butter.

6. In a small bowl, whisk together lime juice, salt, cayenne pepper, and nutritional yeast. Pour over corn, turning to coat. Serve immediately.

BAKED ONION DIP

Remember the onion dip you make from dried onion soup and sour cream, the one that you'd pair with potato chips and devour in one sitting? This one's better. Serve this dip with sliced bread or crackers.

1 large sweet onion, cut in half, peeled, and sliced thin

1 clove garlic, minced

1 teaspoon salt

1 tablespoon olive oil

½ cup vegan mayonnaise

1 (8-ounce) container vegan cream cheese, softened

1 tablespoon dried parsley

1 cup vegan mozzarella shreds

Sliced baguette or crackers

1. Preheat oven to 350°F. Have ready a 1-quart baking dish.

2. In a medium sauté pan over medium-high heat, sauté onions, garlic, and salt in oil until caramelized, about 15 minutes.

3. In a medium bowl, cream mayonnaise and cream cheese, then add parsley and half of mozzarella cheese. Add onion mixture and stir to combine.

4. Spoon into baking dish. Top with remaining mozzarella cheese.

5. Bake 30 minutes or until bubbly and cheese is melted.

POLENTA FRIES

Polenta Fries are a fun party food and great for gluten-free guests. Serve these with Avocado Sauce or Creamy Southwestern Dip (see Chapter 6) or even just ketchup or heated marinara.

1 teaspoon salt

5 cups water

1 cup fine cornmeal

3 tablespoons olive oil, divided

1 tablespoon nutritional yeast

1 tablespoon coarse salt

1. In a large pot, bring salt and water to a rolling boil and whisk in cornmeal, 1 tablespoon olive oil, and nutritional yeast. Turn heat to low and cook until the polenta is very thick, about 25 minutes.

2. Turn polenta out onto a greased baking pan, smooth out, and allow to cool completely.

3. Preheat oven to 375°F.

4. Cut polenta into sticks resembling thick fries, arrange on a baking sheet in a single layer, and drizzle on remaining olive oil and coarse salt. Bake 35–45 minutes until golden and crisp, turning once halfway through baking.

STUFFED MUSHROOMS

» SERVES 6 «

1 pound baby bella mushrooms

¼ cup chopped onions

1 clove garlic, minced

2 tablespoons vegan butter

½ cup vegan cream cheese

1¼ cups bread crumbs, divided

½ teaspoon oregano

½ teaspoon salt

½ teaspoon black pepper

Truly a contrast in textures, these mushrooms give your mouth a pleasant surprise with each bite. Baby bellas add a depth of flavor and hold up nicely to baking, but button mushrooms are readily available and work nicely too. Your choice!

« – »

1. Preheat oven to 375°F. Line a baking sheet with parchment paper.

2. Remove and finely chop mushroom stems.

3. In a medium sauté pan over medium-high heat, sauté mushroom pieces, onions, and garlic in butter until onions are translucent.

4. In a medium bowl, beat cream cheese with a whisk until creamy, then stir in cooked mushroom mixture, ¾ cup bread crumbs, oregano, salt, and pepper.

5. Spoon a heaping teaspoonful of cream cheese mixture into each mushroom cap. Dip cream cheese in ½ cup bread crumbs and place on prepared baking sheet.

6. Bake 8–10 minutes. These can be served hot or at room temperature if you plan to take them to a party.

FALAFEL *with* TAHINI DIP

As far as I'm concerned, falafel should be a food group unto itself. And even though it's deep-fried, it feels healthy, so I consider it a no-guilt junk food. It's super cheap to buy bulk dry garbanzo beans, so this is a good option for the budget-conscious.

« – »

1. Soak chickpeas overnight or at least 6 hours.

2. When ready to cook, in a deep frying pan over medium-high heat, bring about 2" oil to 350°F. On a baking sheet, place crumpled paper towels to drain falafel after they cook.

3. Drain chickpeas and place in a food processor; process until beans are very finely ground.

4. Add onion, garlic, cumin, baking powder, and parsley. Process, adding water a tablespoon at a time until mixture holds together when a spoonful is pressed in your hand.

5. Shape heaping tablespoonfuls of chickpea mix into slightly flattened disks.

6. Cook in preheated oil 3–5 minutes or until golden on both sides. Remove to prepared baking sheet.

7. Serve with Tahini Dip.

Tahini Dip

1. In a small bowl, whisk together tahini and water until smooth.

2. Add lemon juice, salt, and garlic.

3. Keep in an airtight container and use within 3 days.

» SERVES 4 «

1 cup dried chickpeas (garbanzo beans)

Oil (for frying)

2 tablespoons minced onion

1 clove garlic, minced

1 teaspoon cumin

1 teaspoon baking powder

2 tablespoons finely chopped parsley

¼ cup water

½ cup tahini

¼ cup water

2 tablespoons fresh lemon juice

½ teaspoon salt

1 clove garlic, crushed

BEER TEMPURA VEGETABLES

Oil (for frying)

1 (12-ounce) can vegan beer, very cold

2 cups flour

2 teaspoons baking powder

6 cups raw vegetables: broccoli florets, cauliflower florets, red bell pepper slices, yams (thinly sliced lengthwise), green beans, onion slices, button mushrooms, carrot sticks, or zucchini slices

½ cup cornstarch

1 recipe Wasabi Soy Dipping Sauce (see Chapter 6)

Best served hot, these light, crisp veggies have just a hint of beer flavor. Bring them to a party, and you're sure to be invited back time and time again.

« – »

1. In a deep-sided pan over medium-high heat, bring about 3" oil to 350°F. Line a baking sheet with crumpled paper towels to drain cooked vegetables on.

2. In a medium bowl, mix together cold beer, flour, and baking powder until smooth.

3. Dredge vegetables in cornstarch. Dip in batter, allowing excess to drip off.

4. Fry in heated oil 5–7 minutes or until golden brown. Drain on prepared baking sheet.

5. Transfer to a serving plate and set out a small bowl of Wasabi Soy Dipping Sauce for dipping.

SUN-DRIED TOMATO and TURKEY PINWHEELS

1 (8-ounce) container vegan cream cheese

1 (3-ounce) jar oil-packed sun-dried tomatoes, chopped

6 (8") tortillas

2 cups baby spinach

2 (5-ounce) packages vegan turkey deli slices

Don't let the spinach in this recipe fool you; these are more delicious than they are healthy. Plus, they whip up in a matter of minutes, and you can easily double or triple the recipe if you're expecting a horde of friends at your house!

« – »

1. In a small bowl, mix cream cheese and sun-dried tomatoes until smooth.

2. On each tortilla, spread a heaping tablespoonful of cream cheese mixture evenly with a rubber spatula. Arrange spinach on top of cream cheese, followed by deli slices.

3. Roll into a tight cylinder. Cut each cylinder into 1½" wheels. Refrigerate until ready to eat.

SAUSAGE PUFFS

This really is the ultimate junk food. Not only do you have super-salty sausage mixed with onion, mayo, and bread crumbs, but you fold it all in a decadent, flaky puff pastry. Expect to be asked for this recipe if you serve it at brunch.

½ medium onion, peeled and chopped

1 (6-ounce) package vegan Lightlife Gimme Lean Sausage

1 tablespoon oil

1 tablespoon dried parsley

1 cup bread crumbs

¼ cup vegan mayonnaise

1 (17.3-ounce) package puff pastry sheets (Pepperidge Farm brand is vegan)

1. Preheat oven to 350°F. Line a baking sheet with parchment paper.

2. In a medium sauté pan over medium-high heat, cook onion and sausage in oil, breaking sausage up into small pieces. Cook until sausage and onion are lightly browned. Remove from heat, transfer to a medium bowl, and cool completely before next step.

3. Add parsley and bread crumbs to the cooled sausage mixture. Stir in mayonnaise.

4. On a large cutting board using a sharp knife, cut pastry sheet lengthwise so that you have two long rectangles of dough. Place dough on prepared baking sheet.

5. Place half of sausage mixture in a long row down the middle of each dough rectangle.

6. Fold dough over sausage, making a long, skinny rectangle. Crimp open edges closed with a fork. Cut into 2"-wide slices. Separate lightly on a cookie sheet.

7. Bake 15–20 minutes or until very golden brown.

TERIYAKI PINEAPPLE CHICKEN KABOBS

Aside from the straight salty or straight saccharine, most junk food shares the common bond of having a savory and sweet flavor profile. On display here is a terrific example, inspired by the islands.

» SERVES 4 «

1 recipe Pineapple Teriyaki Sauce (see Chapter 6)

1 (9-ounce) package Beyond Meat Beyond Chicken Strips, cubed

Wooden skewers, soaked in water 15 minutes

2 cups cubed fresh pineapple

2 cups cherry tomatoes

1 small red onion, peeled and cut into large chunks

2 tablespoons olive oil

1. Preheat oven to 400°F. Line a baking sheet with parchment paper. Or heat your barbecue if grilling.

2. In a medium bowl, toss Pineapple Teriyaki Sauce and chicken, then marinate 2 hours in the refrigerator.

3. On each skewer, alternate chicken, pineapple, cherry tomatoes, and onions. Place on prepared baking sheet.

4. Brush vegetables with Pineapple Teriyaki Sauce and olive oil.

5. Bake 20 minutes or until onions are tender.

6. To grill: brush grate with oil and grill 10–12 minutes, turning once halfway through cooking.

BUFFALO CAULIFLOWER DIP

1 small head cauliflower, chopped

1 (12-ounce) bottle Frank's RedHot sauce

2 (8-ounce) containers vegan cream cheese

1 recipe Creamy Ranch Dressing (see Chapter 6)

¾ cup chopped celery

1 cup vegan mozzarella shreds

6 ribs celery, cut into large sticks

1 French bread baguette

I present a creamy, cheesy, hot sauce–infused dip with cauliflower chunks, best enjoyed piping hot with celery sticks or a hunk of crusty French bread.

1. Preheat oven to 350°F. Lightly grease 9" × 13" baking dish.

2. In baking dish, mix cauliflower with hot sauce.

3. In a small bowl, mix cream cheese and Creamy Ranch Dressing with celery and pour over cauliflower mixture.

4. Cover tightly with foil.

5. Bake 20 minutes, remove foil, and top with cheese shreds.

6. Bake an additional 15–20 minutes or until shreds are melted.

7. Serve with celery sticks and French bread torn into chunks.

EGGPLANT CAVIAR

1 large eggplant

2 cloves garlic

¾ cup Vegan Sour Cream (see Chapter 6)

1 tablespoon fresh lemon juice

1 teaspoon salt

½ teaspoon black pepper

Pita chips

It feels particularly festive to tell someone, "Oh, I'll bring a side of Eggplant Caviar!" even though this recipe technically has very little in common with actual caviar (which is fish roe). No matter! Junk food is all about the fun factor, so I'm sticking to it.

1. Preheat oven to 350°F. Cut eggplant in half lengthwise, place cut side down on parchment-lined cookie sheet, and place a clove of garlic under each side. Bake 40 minutes or until very soft.

2. When cool enough to handle, spoon eggplant out of skin and roughly chop with garlic.

3. In a medium bowl, mix Vegan Sour Cream, lemon juice, salt, and pepper. Stir in eggplant.

4. Serve with pita chips and be sure to refrigerate leftovers.

BEER-BARBECUED MEATBALLS

Let someone else serve Swedish meatballs; I'd rather put out these happy little vegan balls cooked in a beer-infused barbecue marinade. The best part? Gobbling them up with toothpicks. You can use premade vegan meatballs in a pinch, but here's how to do it from scratch.

1 (8-ounce) package tempeh, crumbled

2 tablespoons ground flaxseeds

¼ cup water

½ medium onion, peeled and diced

1 teaspoon olive oil

1 clove garlic, chopped

1 tablespoon tomato paste

1 teaspoon vegan Worcestershire sauce

1 teaspoon light soy sauce

½ cup bread crumbs

½ cup walnuts, finely minced

½ teaspoon oregano

½ teaspoon parsley

½ teaspoon basil

1 (12-ounce) can vegan beer

2 cups barbecue sauce

1. Preheat oven to 350°F. Line a baking sheet with parchment paper.

2. Steam crumbled tempeh in a steamer basket over boiling water 15 minutes.

3. In a small bowl, mix flaxseeds with water; set aside.

4. In a medium sauté pan over medium heat, cook onions in oil, stirring until translucent, about 5 minutes; add garlic, sauté 1 more minute. Remove from heat.

5. In a large bowl, combine all the ingredients except the beer and barbecue sauce and mix with hands until very well combined. If mixture is too dry to be shaped into a ball, add 1 more tablespoon tomato paste. If mixture is too wet, add bread crumbs ¼ cup at a time until you can easily shape into 1½" balls.

6. Place balls on prepared baking sheet.

7. Bake 25–30 minutes, carefully turning meatballs halfway through cooking. Meatballs are done when deep golden brown.

8. In a large saucepan, mix beer and barbecue sauce, add meatballs, and bring to a boil. Turn heat down to medium-low and let simmer 15–20 minutes.

9. Serve on a serving platter with toothpicks and extra sauce in a small bowl.

TAQUITOS *with* AVOCADO SAUCE

2 large potatoes, peeled and chopped

1 (12-ounce) package Soyrizo vegan Mexican sausage (about 1 cup)

1 teaspoon salt

1 teaspoon cumin

8 corn tortillas

3 tablespoons oil

1 recipe Avocado Sauce (see Chapter 6)

Fry these taquitos and you're well on the way to making an irresistible junk food.

« – »

1. Line a baking sheet with crumpled paper towels for draining cooked taquitos.

2. In a medium saucepan, bring enough salted water to boil to cover potatoes. Cook potatoes until fork-tender. Remove from heat and drain.

3. In a medium sauté pan over medium-high heat, cook Soyrizo, stirring frequently, 4 minutes. Add salt, cumin, and potatoes to the pan and stir to combine. Remove from heat.

4. In a large dry sauté pan over medium heat, heat corn tortillas on each side just until soft. Keep warm wrapped in a clean kitchen towel.

5. Preheat a large frying pan over medium-high heat; add about 3 tablespoons oil to pan.

6. For each taquito, spoon a heaping tablespoon of potato mixture into each tortilla and spread evenly. Roll and secure with a toothpick.

7. Fry in heated oil (toothpick and all) about 2 minutes on each side or until evenly golden brown. Place on prepared baking sheet to drain.

8. Serve with Avocado Sauce.

PIZZA ROLLS

1½ cups Super-Easy Pizza Sauce (see Chapter 4)

1 cup vegan pepperoni, finely chopped

1 cup vegan mozzarella shreds

1 (12-ounce) package vegan wonton wrappers

Oil (for frying)

Pizza toppings deep-fried in a wonton wrapper equal junk food bliss.

« – »

1. In a large frying pan, heat about 2" oil to 360°F. Line a baking sheet with crumpled paper towels to drain cooked pizza rolls.

2. In a medium bowl, mix Super-Easy Pizza Sauce, pepperoni, and cheese.

3. Brush edges of wonton wrapper with water; place a scant teaspoon of pizza sauce mixture on wonton and fold over, pressing edge to seal completely.

4. Fry pizza rolls in oil on each side 2–3 minutes or until golden brown. Place on prepared baking sheet to drain.

GREEN CHILI WHITE BEAN QUESADILLA

1 (15-ounce) can cannellini beans, rinsed and drained

1½ cups vegan mozzarella shreds

1 (14-ounce) can diced green chilies

1 teaspoon salt

1 teaspoon cumin

4–6 (6") flour tortillas

1 teaspoon oil

1 recipe Creamy Southwestern Dip (see Chapter 6)

White beans add the perfect texture to this protein-filled snack staple.

« – »

1. In a small bowl, mash beans with a potato masher until mostly smooth; stir in cheese, chilies, salt, and cumin.

2. Spoon a heaping tablespoonful of the spread on ½ of a tortilla and fold over. Continue for rest of tortillas.

3. In a large sauté pan over medium-high heat, heat a thin layer of oil and cook quesadillas until lightly browned and crisp, about 4 minutes. Cut into triangles and serve with Creamy Southwestern Dip.

ZUCCHINI PANCAKES

Know how to turn the glut of zucchinis from your garden into bona fide junk food? Turn them into pancakes and deep-fry those suckers! A real crowd favorite.

« ------------------------------------ »

1. Grate zucchini, toss with salt, and place in a colander to drain, about 20 minutes.

2. In a medium frying pan, heat about 1" oil over medium-high heat to about 360°F. Line a baking sheet with crumpled paper towels to drain cooked pancakes on.

3. In a small bowl, combine flaxseeds with water. Set aside.

4. Place zucchini and onion in a kitchen towel and squeeze excess moisture out.

5. In a medium bowl, mix zucchini, onion, flaxseed mixture, cornmeal, flour, and pepper.

6. Place a heaping tablespoon of zucchini mixture into prepared oil, flattening slightly with a spatula.

7. Fry 3–4 minutes on each side or until golden brown. Remove and place on prepared baking sheet to drain.

8. Serve while still warm with a side of Vegan Sour Cream.

>> SERVES 4 «

2 medium-sized zucchinis

1 teaspoon salt

Oil (for frying)

1 teaspoon ground flaxseeds

1 tablespoon water

4 tablespoons grated onion

¼ cup cornmeal

¼ cup flour

½ teaspoon black pepper

1 cup Vegan Sour Cream (see Chapter 6)

HAM-WRAPPED ASPARAGUS *with* CHIVE CREAM CHEESE

1 bunch asparagus spears
(10–12 spears)

1 (8-ounce) container vegan
cream cheese

1 teaspoon Dijon mustard

1 tablespoon minced fresh
chives

½ teaspoon salt

1 (5-ounce) package vegan
deli slices

How do you turn asparagus into junk food? Wrap it in cream cheese and ham, that's how.

« – »

1. Bring a quart of salted water to boil in a pan that will accommodate asparagus spears.

2. Snap off woody ends of asparagus. Add asparagus to boiling water. Cook 3–5 minutes or until cooked through but not mushy. Remove from heat and drain; run cold water over asparagus to stop spears from overcooking. Set aside to cool.

3. In a small bowl, combine cream cheese, mustard, chives, and salt.

4. On each deli slice, spread a heaping teaspoonful of cream cheese mixture evenly.

5. Roll deli slice around a spear of asparagus. Set on a serving platter and repeat for rest of spears. Refrigerate until ready to serve.

JALAPEÑO BACON POPPERS

Nonvegans would look at this recipe title and think, "Bacon? What's up with that?" Fortunately, several manufacturers have specialized in veganizing our junk food favorites, namely cheese and meat stuffs, so we, too, can enjoy crispy fried poppers with a molten creamy bacony filling.

‹‹ – ››

1. In a large frying pan, heat about 2"–3" oil over medium-high heat; oil should be between 350°F and 375°F. Line a baking sheet with crumpled paper towels to drain cooked poppers on.

2. In a small bowl, mix cream cheese, cheese, and bacon.

3. Using gloves to protect fingers from seeds, slice jalapeños lengthwise and discard seeds and veins.

4. In three separate shallow bowls, place cornstarch, milk, and flour mixed with bread crumbs and salt.

5. Spoon a heaping teaspoonful of cream cheese mixture into each jalapeño half.

6. Dredge poppers in cornstarch, then milk, then bread crumb mixture. Lay them on a sheet of parchment paper. Re-dredge in milk and bread crumbs.

7. Fry poppers in batches in prepared oil 3–5 minutes or until golden. Set poppers on prepared baking sheet to drain.

8. Transfer to a serving platter and serve while still piping hot. Yum!

» **SERVES 4–6** «

Oil (for frying)

1 (8-ounce) container vegan cream cheese

1½ cups vegan Cheddar shreds

1 (6-ounce) package Lightlife Organic Fakin' Bacon Smoky Tempeh Strips, chopped

10 large jalapeño peppers

½ cup cornstarch

1 cup nondairy milk

½ cup flour

1 cup fine bread crumbs

1 teaspoon salt

LOADED NACHOS

A staple for your next vegan football gathering, or any time you have a hankering for a heap of tortilla chips smothered in spicy jackfruit, refried beans, and jalapeño; baked until the cheese gets all melty; and topped with a generous dollop of tomatoes, guac, and sour cream. Classic.

« – »

1. In a medium sauté pan over medium heat, cook jackfruit with onions in oil until jackfruit begins to fall apart, about 15 minutes; use two forks to help pull into threads. Add chili powder, cumin, pepper, and garlic powder, stirring until mixed well and fragrant. Remove from heat.

2. Preheat oven to 375°F. Have a large ovenproof platter or 9" × 13" baking dish ready.

3. In a small saucepan, heat refried beans with milk, stirring until heated through. Remove from heat.

4. Place tortilla chips on the platter or baking dish in an even double layer.

5. Spoon beans over chips, followed by jackfruit mixture, cheese, and jalapeños.

6. Bake 8–10 minutes or until cheese is melted.

7. Top nachos with green onion, cilantro, guacamole, Vegan Sour Cream, and diced tomato.

>> SERVES 4 <<

- 1 (14-ounce) can green jackfruit in brine, drained well
- ½ medium onion, peeled and chopped
- 1 tablespoon oil
- 1 teaspoon chili powder
- 1 teaspoon cumin
- ½ teaspoon black pepper
- ½ teaspoon garlic powder
- 1 (15-ounce) can refried pinto beans
- ¼ cup nondairy milk
- 12 ounces tortilla chips
- 1 cup vegan Cheddar shreds
- 1 medium jalapeño, seeded and sliced
- 3 green onions, white and green parts, sliced thinly
- ¼ cup chopped cilantro
- 1 cup guacamole
- 1 cup Vegan Sour Cream (see Chapter 6)
- 1 medium tomato, seeded and diced

BARBECUE CHIP-CRUSTED TOFU BITES

» SERVES 4–6 «

Oil (for frying)

1 (16-ounce) package extra-firm tofu, drained, frozen, and then thawed

½ cup cornstarch

¾ cup flour

½ teaspoon baking powder

1 cup ice water

1 cup barbecue potato chips, crushed

1 recipe Creamy Ranch Dressing (see Chapter 6)

Ready for the crunchiest tofu you've ever had? Blame potato chips and deep-frying for the delicious result.

« – »

1. In a large, deep pan, heat about 3" oil to 345°F.

2. Cut tofu into 1" cubes.

3. Place cornstarch in a plastic bag large enough to hold tofu.

4. In a medium bowl, combine flour, baking powder, and ice water. Stir to make a thick batter; do not overmix. A few lumps are okay.

5. Pour barbecue chips into a shallow dish.

6. Place tofu into bag with cornstarch and shake to evenly coat tofu cubes.

7. A few at a time, dip tofu cubes into batter, letting excess drip off, then roll in barbecue chip crumbs.

8. Carefully place tofu into heated oil and fry about 2 minutes. Remove to paper towels to drain.

9. Transfer to a groovy serving platter and put out a side of Creamy Ranch Dressing to encourage dipping.

TOFU SATAY *with* WASABI SOY DIPPING SAUCE

Aside from being packed with protein, tofu takes on the flavor of just about anything, making it an almost magical food and a vegan staple. In this recipe, the longer you're able to marinade the tofu, the more flavor you'll pack into your satay.

» SERVES 4 «

1 tablespoon finely chopped lemongrass

1 tablespoon grated ginger

1 clove garlic, crushed

1 tablespoon agave

1 tablespoon chili sauce, or 1 red chili seeded and thinly sliced (optional)

½ teaspoon sesame oil

3 tablespoons light soy sauce

1 (12-ounce) package extra-firm tofu, drained, frozen, thawed, and cut into even bite-sized squares

Wooden skewers soaked in water 15 minutes

4 tablespoons olive oil

1 recipe Wasabi Soy Dipping Sauce (see Chapter 6)

1. In a shallow dish, combine lemongrass, ginger, garlic, agave, chili sauce (if using), sesame oil, and soy sauce.

2. Add tofu chunks, turning to coat in marinade. Refrigerate for a few hours or overnight, stirring to make sure all the tofu stays coated in the marinade.

3. Preheat oven to 300°F. If barbecuing, heat your grill. Place 4 or 5 pieces of tofu on each skewer, place on a cookie sheet, and brush with olive oil.

4. Bake 40 minutes, turning each skewer every 15 minutes.

5. To cook on the grill: brush the grate with oil and cook 10–12 minutes, turning once halfway through cooking.

6. Serve with a generous side of Wasabi Soy Dipping Sauce for dipping.

CORN FRITTERS

½ cup soy milk

1 teaspoon apple cider vinegar

¾ cup flour

1 teaspoon baking powder

¼ teaspoon salt

¼ teaspoon baking soda

⅛ teaspoon paprika

1 tablespoon oil

1 cup frozen corn kernels,
    thawed and drained

Oil (for frying)

We've taken a detour to the Deep South with this deep-fried treasure. Double the deliciousness if you've got a crowd to feed. For a real down-home feast, serve with a side of vegan ribs, crunchy slaw, and a pitcher of spiked lemonade.

1. Place soy milk and apple cider vinegar in a small bowl and set aside 5 minutes.

2. In a medium bowl, combine flour, baking powder, salt, baking soda, and paprika.

3. Add 1 tablespoon oil to milk mixture. Stir wet ingredients into dry ingredients until just combined, then add corn.

4. Heat about 1" oil in a pan and drop in fritters by the heaping tablespoonful. Fry on each side until golden, about 4 minutes.

5. Drain on paper towels before setting out to serve. Add a generous smear of vegan butter for the yummiest results.

CHAPTER 6

Dips for All Seasons

...and All Reasons

HOMEMADE KETCHUP

1 large onion, peeled and chopped

2 tablespoons olive oil

4 cloves garlic, chopped

1 (28-ounce) can whole tomatoes

1 (28-ounce) can tomato paste

3 teaspoons mustard powder

1 teaspoon allspice

1 teaspoon ground clove

1 teaspoon ground cinnamon

¼ teaspoon cayenne pepper

1 cup packed light-brown sugar

½ cup apple cider vinegar

2 tablespoons molasses

A lot of ingredients, yes, but this handy condiment cooks up fast and packs a serious flavor punch! You'll never want store-bought ketchup again.

« – »

1. In a medium sauté pan over medium-high heat, cook onions in olive oil until just beginning to caramelize, about 8 minutes. Add garlic and cook until fragrant, about 3 minutes.

2. Place whole tomatoes in a blender and add cooked onions and garlic. Blend until smooth.

3. In a large heavy-bottomed stockpot, combine all ingredients over medium-high heat until ketchup begins to boil. Turn down to low, partially cover, and cook until extremely thick, about 1 hour, stirring constantly to prevent scorching.

4. Spoon finished ketchup into canning jars; allow to cool completely on the counter before refrigerating.

VEGAN RICOTTA

Look here when you want to make such staples as lasagna or stuffed shells. (And see if you can fool your Italian grandma!)

» MAKES 2 CUPS «

8 ounces firm tofu, crumbled into tiny pieces

1 (8-ounce) container vegan cream cheese, softened

1 tablespoon lemon juice

2 tablespoons nutritional yeast

1 teaspoon dried parsley

1 teaspoon salt

« - »

1. In a medium bowl, stir together tofu and cream cheese with a whisk until well combined.

2. Add lemon juice, nutritional yeast, parsley, and salt. Refrigerate overnight for best results.

VEGAN SOUR CREAM

This is so easy to whip up, there's no need to go the store-bought route: a vegan staple that is tangy, cool, and creamy.

» MAKES ABOUT 2 CUPS «

1 (16-ounce) package silken tofu

4 tablespoons oil

4 tablespoons lemon juice

1 teaspoon salt

« - »

1. Mix tofu, oil, lemon juice, and salt in a food processor or blender until very smooth. Taste for correct tartness and add more lemon juice if necessary.

2. Store in the fridge when not using.

CUMIN YOGURT

1½ cups coconut yogurt, unsweetened

1 teaspoon cumin

2 teaspoons lemon zest

2 cloves garlic

1 tablespoon olive oil

3–4 fresh basil leaves

1 teaspoon salt

½ teaspoon black pepper

This spiced yogurt sauce is at its best drizzled over grilled slabs of summer vegetables.

1. Place all ingredients in a food processor and mix until well blended.

2. Refrigerate overnight.

HARISSA

4 ounces mixed dried chilies, stemmed and seeded (any variety New Mexico, arbol, guajillo, chipotle, or ancho)

¼ teaspoon caraway

½ teaspoon coriander seed

1 teaspoon cumin

4 cloves garlic

1 teaspoon salt

This Tunisian condiment gets its flavor from chilies, and it's perfect on roasted carrots, stirred into hummus, or as a base layer spread for sandwiches.

1. In a heat-proof bowl, cover chilies with boiling water and allow to sit until chilies are soft, about 20 minutes. Drain well.

2. Place chilies and all other ingredients in a food processor and mix until everything is smooth.

3. Keep refrigerated.

CHEESE SAUCE

It's vegan Velveeta! In this clever fake-out, the vegetables provide body and color, and the result is a thick, rich sauce with lots of mild cheese flavor. Generously pour this sauce over pasta, potatoes, broccoli, or nachos.

- 1 medium potato, peeled and chopped into 2" pieces
- 4 medium carrots, chopped into 2" pieces
- ¼ head cauliflower, chopped into 2" pieces
- 2 cups vegetable broth
- 1 cup nutritional yeast
- 1 (8-ounce) container vegan cream cheese
- 1 teaspoon Dijon mustard
- 1 teaspoon turmeric
- 1 teaspoon onion powder
- ¼ cup vegan butter
- ¼ cup flour
- 2 cups nondairy milk

1. In a large saucepan over high heat, bring potato, carrots, cauliflower, and broth to a boil, then cover and turn the heat down to low. Cook until vegetables are very soft, about 10–12 minutes. Drain.

2. Place vegetables in a food processor and process until they become smooth. Add nutritional yeast, cream cheese, mustard, turmeric, and onion powder.

3. Pour mixture into a large saucepan over medium-high heat.

4. In a small bowl, blend butter and flour together to make a paste. When mixture in the saucepan comes to a boil, whisk in butter-flour mixture. Whisk in milk and allow mixture to cook until to desired thickness. Remove from heat.

BALSAMIC REDUCTION

1 bottle balsamic vinegar
(about 12 ounces)

¼ cup brown sugar

Here's a staple you don't know you're missing until you have it on hand to drizzle over pizza or a salad. Sweet and slightly tart, Balsamic Reduction wakes up everything it touches, from sandwiches, to roasted vegetables, to ice cream, and beyond.

« – »

1. In a medium saucepan over medium-high heat, bring balsamic vinegar to a boil and stir in brown sugar.

2. Reduce heat to medium; cook 15–20 minutes. Note where the balsamic vinegar reaches the side of the pan; you want it to reduce down until you have 25 percent of what you started with.

3. When it's done, the reduction will be thick enough to coat the back of a spoon.

PINEAPPLE TERIYAKI SAUCE

3 tablespoons cornstarch

1 cup soy sauce

1 (20-ounce) can chunk
pineapple (packed in
100 percent pineapple
juice)

½ cup packed brown sugar

1 teaspoon chopped garlic

A sweet, salty, thick marinade that makes anything it comes in contact with a special treat.

« – »

1. In a small bowl, whisk cornstarch into the soy sauce.

2. Add all ingredients to a medium saucepan and bring to a boil. Simmer until sauce thickens, about 10–15 minutes.

SPICY PEANUT SAUCE

Addicted to the peanut sauce at the Thai place down the street? Now you can re-create it in the comfort of your own home—and slather it on anything you please!

«------------------------------------»

1. In a large bowl, combine all the ingredients using a whisk, tasting for a balance of hot and sweet.

2. Refrigerate in an airtight container and use within 4 days.

» MAKES 1½ CUPS «

¾ cup peanut butter, creamy or chunky

¼ cup lime juice

1 medium jalapeño, seeded for less heat, minced

½ cup seasoned rice vinegar

¼ cup brown sugar

2 tablespoons finely chopped cilantro

½ teaspoon salt

WASABI SOY DIPPING SAUCE

Try to get your hands on low-sodium soy sauce for this recipe; otherwise, the sauce can become overpowered by the saltiness. Want to ratchet up the heat? Increase the amount of wasabi paste. This is a great dipping sauce for egg rolls and wontons, or mixed into rice.

«------------------------------------»

1. In a medium bowl, whisk together soy sauce and vinegar. Add wasabi 1 teaspoon at a time to desired heat.

2. Keep leftover sauce in the refrigerator and use within 2 days.

» MAKES ABOUT 1 CUP «

½ cup low-sodium soy sauce

¼ cup seasoned rice vinegar

2 teaspoons wasabi paste

BASIL PESTO

⅓ cup pine nuts

2 cups fresh basil

2 cloves garlic

¼ cup nutritional yeast

1 teaspoon salt

½ cup extra-virgin olive oil

Pesto, presto! Whip up a batch of this versatile condiment with all sorts of variations. It's delicious when simply slathered on a slice of fresh crusty bread.

« – »

1. In a food processor, add pine nuts and basil; process until basil is finely chopped. Add garlic, nutritional yeast, and salt. Drizzle in olive oil while machine is running.

2. Refrigerate leftovers in an airtight container and use within 5 days.

Sun-Dried Tomato Pesto

Add a 3-ounce bag of whole sun-dried tomatoes to the food processor with the basil.

Cilantro Pesto

Add 2 cups fresh cilantro instead of the basil, and add walnuts instead of pine nuts. Omit the nutritional yeast and add in a teaspoon of finely chopped jalapeño.

EASY SALSA FRESCA

Quick-to-put-together salsa but with all the flavor of a great salsa, this pairs well with tofu scramble or tortilla chips when a snack attack hits.

« – »

Combine all ingredients and refrigerate for a few hours to develop flavors. Use within 4 days.

» MAKES ABOUT
2 CUPS «

2 medium tomatoes, seeded and chopped

1 medium jalapeño pepper, seeded and chopped

¼ cup chopped onion

¼ cup finely chopped cilantro

Juice of 1 medium lime

1 teaspoon salt

AVOCADO SAUCE

Because it's so much thinner than guacamole, sometimes I think this recipe wants to be a chilled soup, and I would eat it that way in a heartbeat. But for the purposes of this book—and because the buttery flavor of avocado takes a back seat to the bite of jalapeño and fresh notes of lime and cilantro—consider how to incorporate this street taco condiment into your Mexican-inspired dishes.

« – »

1. In a blender, blend all ingredients, adding water about a ¼ cup at a time to make a somewhat-thin sauce.

2. Keeps in the refrigerator 2 days.

» MAKES ABOUT
1½ CUPS «

2 medium avocados

1 medium jalapeño (or 1 serrano pepper, depending on heat desired), seeded

1 tablespoon fresh lime juice

1 teaspoon salt

2–3 sprigs cilantro

⅛ medium onion, peeled and finely chopped

½–1 cup water

CREAMY SOUTHWESTERN DIP

Need a dip for tortilla chips or to dollop on top of your vegan chili? Look no further: this creamy salsa fresca will do the trick.

» MAKES 2 CUPS «

1 medium tomato, seeded and diced small

¼ cup finely chopped cilantro

1 medium jalapeño, seeded and finely minced

⅛ medium onion, finely minced

1 teaspoon dried parsley

½ teaspoon salt

¼ teaspoon ground cumin

1 cup Vegan Sour Cream (see recipe in this chapter)

½ cup vegan mayonnaise

1. In a medium bowl, combine all ingredients. Whisk the mixture until smooth. Refrigerate at least 1 hour so that the dip firms up a bit before serving.

2. Store leftovers in an airtight container and use within 4 days.

SPINACH ARTICHOKE DIP

There's a reason no one wants to move away from this stuff at a party. It's ridiculously rich and creamy! Be sure to serve while piping hot for yummiest results.

» SERVES 6 «

1 (10-ounce) package frozen spinach, thawed and chopped

1 (14-ounce) can artichoke hearts, drained and chopped

1 cup vegan mayonnaise

1 (8-ounce) container vegan cream cheese

½ cup Vegan Sour Cream (see recipe in this chapter)

¼ cup nutritional yeast

½ teaspoon garlic powder

½ teaspoon onion powder

1 teaspoon salt

½ teaspoon black pepper

⅛ teaspoon cayenne pepper

1 cup vegan mozzarella shreds

1. Preheat oven to 350°F. Mix all ingredients except mozzarella shreds in a 2-quart casserole dish. Top with mozzarella.

2. Bake 20–25 minutes or until bubbly and just starting to brown.

3. Serve with French bread pieces or tortilla chips. Surely, there won't be leftovers.

CREAMY RANCH DRESSING

» MAKES 1 CUP «

½ cup finely ground saltine crackers

½ cup dried parsley

1 tablespoon dried minced onion

1 teaspoon dried chives

1 tablespoon garlic powder

1 teaspoon onion powder

2 teaspoons salt

1 teaspoon black pepper

½ cup vegan mayonnaise

½ cup Vegan Sour Cream (see recipe in this chapter)

¼ cup soy milk

Oniony, creamy, and rich—I find that this dressing adds a bit of life to almost all foods, and it can definitely turn some foods junky! (Prep the dry ingredients and keep the mixture on hand for whenever you need to pull together a dressing in a jiffy.)

1. To make the Creamy Ranch Dressing mix: combine all the dry ingredients and store in plastic container. Makes about 1 cup.

2. To make a dip with the Creamy Ranch Dressing mix: combine 1 tablespoon dressing mix, vegan mayonnaise, and Vegan Sour Cream.

3. To use the dip as a dressing for salad: stir in soy milk to thin. Refrigerate at least 1 hour before using.

4. Store in an airtight container and use within 5 days.

SWEET *and* TANGY BACON DRESSING

» MAKES 2¼ CUPS «

2 teaspoons oil

¼ medium onion, peeled and chopped

2 tablespoons vegan bacon bits, such as Frontier Co-Op Organic Bac'Uns Vegetarian Bits

¼ cup sugar

¼ cup apple cider vinegar

¼ cup water

2 cups vegan mayonnaise

Your Savory Twice-Baked Potatoes (see Chapter 3) are begging for this! Don't let them down!

1. In a medium sauté pan over medium-high heat, sauté onions in oil until they turn golden and are very soft, about 10 minutes. Add bacon bits and stir.

2. Stir in sugar, vinegar, and water, and bring to a boil, stirring constantly. Cook until sugar is melted and mixture boils 2 full minutes. Remove from heat and cool before the next step.

3. In a medium bowl, whisk cooled onion mixture with the mayonnaise until completely combined. Refrigerate.

CAESAR SALAD DRESSING

While not an authentic Caesar, this has all the right elements of tang, creaminess, and garlic flavor with a hint of cheese from the nutritional yeast. (Plus, who really likes sardines, anyhow?)

» MAKES 1½ CUPS «

1 cup raw almonds, soaked overnight

¼ cup lemon juice

¼ cup vegan mayonnaise

3 tablespoons olive oil

¼ cup water

1 tablespoon nutritional yeast

2 cloves garlic

1 teaspoon salt

½ teaspoon vegan Worcestershire sauce

½ teaspoon black pepper

1. Drain almonds and put in a food processor with lemon juice, mayonnaise, and oil. Process while adding water 1 tablespoon at a time until mixture is wet enough to process into a creamy salad-dressing consistency.

2. Add nutritional yeast, garlic, salt, Worcestershire sauce, and pepper. Process until smooth.

3. Store in an airtight container and use within 4 days.

PIZZA HUMMUS

No time to make an actual pizza? Take the quickest route to satisfying your urge with this cheesy, tomato-y spread.

» MAKES 2 CUPS «

1 (3-ounce) package sun-dried tomatoes

1 (15-ounce) can garbanzo beans, drained and rinsed

½ cup nutritional yeast

¼ cup olive oil

2 tablespoons lemon juice

2 cloves garlic

1 teaspoon basil

1 teaspoon oregano

½ teaspoon parsley

½ teaspoon salt

2 tablespoons water

1 (4-ounce) package Lightlife Smart Deli Veggie Pepperoni Slices, chopped

1. Combine all ingredients except pepperoni in a food processor and process until very smooth, adding a few tablespoons more water if needed to help blend. Spoon into a serving bowl and stir in pepperoni.

2. Serve with toasted pita or chunks of French bread.

3. Store in an airtight container in the refrigerator and use within 4 days.

GREEN CHILI DIP

» MAKES ABOUT
2 CUPS «

½ cup vegan mayonnaise

1 (8-ounce) container vegan cream cheese

1 (4-ounce) can diced green chilies

1 (4-ounce) can diced jalapeño

1 teaspoon garlic salt

2 tablespoons lemon juice

½ teaspoon black pepper

I learned this recipe from the family I babysat for as a teen, and it's gone through many incarnations over the years until finally going vegan. It is the absolute best served with a big bowl of Fritos.

1. Combine all ingredients with whisk until smooth. Refrigerate for a few hours before serving.

2. Store in the refrigerator and use within 4 days.

CHIPOTLE BEAN DIP

» MAKES ABOUT
2 CUPS «

2–3 whole chipotle chilies in adobo sauce

1 teaspoon oil

½ small onion, peeled and chopped

½ teaspoon salt

½ teaspoon cumin

1 (15-ounce) can black beans, drained and rinsed

1 cup Vegan Sour Cream (see recipe in this chapter)

¼ cup chopped cilantro

Juice of 1 medium lime

Here's a complex bean dip that probably fits in better on the menu at a hip restaurant than it does in a cookbook glorifying junk food, but you can dress it up or dress it down according to your needs. Pair with pita chips—or tortilla chips.

1. Put chilies in food processor and process until they become a paste.

2. In a medium nonstick pan over medium heat, heat oil and sauté onion until translucent, about 5 minutes. Add salt and cumin to the pan and cook until the spice becomes aromatic, about 20 seconds.

3. Add onion mixture and beans to the food processor and process until smooth.

4. Add Vegan Sour Cream, cilantro, and lime juice, and process until combined.

5. Store in the refrigerator and use within 4 days.

BASIC HUMMUS

In my house, we always have a batch of homemade hummus in the fridge, because you just never know when a craving for creamy Mediterranean goodness will strike. It takes all of 6 minutes to make, so it's no hassle to keep us stocked. If you're unfamiliar with tahini, it's a roasted sesame-seed paste normally found with international foods at the market. Be sure to stir tahini really well before you use it.

» MAKES 2 CUPS «

- 1 (15-ounce) can garbanzo beans, drained and rinsed
- 3 tablespoons water
- 3 tablespoons olive oil
- 3 teaspoons tahini
- 2 tablespoons fresh lemon juice
- 1 teaspoon salt

1. In a food processor, combine garbanzo beans, water, oil, tahini, lemon juice, and salt. Process until very smooth, about 4 minutes.

2. Add-ins: garlic, jalapeño, roasted eggplant, roasted red peppers, paprika, toasted pine nuts, cilantro, basil, or chipotle peppers.

3. Store in an airtight container in the refrigerator and use within 4 days.

GARLIC CHIVE DIP

You may want to plan on chowing down on this when you don't have to talk to anyone important afterward... your breath is likely to be a wee bit smelly. (Totally worth it.)

» MAKES 1½ CUPS «

- 1½ cups Vegan Sour Cream (see recipe in this chapter)
- 1 tablespoon minced fresh chives
- 1 tablespoon minced fresh parsley
- 2 cloves garlic, minced
- 1 teaspoon celery salt
- 1 teaspoon dried minced onion
- ½ teaspoon black pepper

1. In a small bowl, combine Vegan Sour Cream, chives, parsley, garlic, celery salt, onion, and pepper; mix until well combined. Refrigerate overnight.

2. Use within 4 days.

TIPSY CARAMEL SAUCE

½ cup soy creamer

½ cup vegan butter

1 cup brown sugar

1 teaspoon salt

1 tablespoon bourbon

Sweet and thick with a hint of bourbon, this spiked version marries nicely with breakfast stuffs (think pancakes or waffles), although I've been known to dip cookies into it!

1. In a large saucepan over medium-high heat, bring soy creamer, butter, brown sugar, and salt to a full boil, whisking constantly. Turn heat down to medium-low and continue to whisk and cook until sauce begins to thicken about 6 minutes. Remove from heat and stir in bourbon.

2. Serve warmed on vegan ice cream or on top of apple pie. Refrigerate leftovers.

LENTIL WALNUT PÂTÉ

» SERVES 6 «

1 cup raw walnuts

1 tablespoon olive oil

1 large onion, peeled and chopped

1 clove garlic

1 cup brown lentils, cooked in a quart of water for 40 minutes, drained

2 teaspoons soy sauce

1 teaspoon balsamic vinegar

½ cup water

This recipe may seem highbrow, but it's more about decadence. Splurge on some of the most buttery vegan crackers you can get your hands on, set out a plate of high-quality olives, and revel in the indulgence of it all!

1. Place walnuts in a medium sauté pan and toast over medium heat. Walnuts are done when they just begin to turn golden and smell fragrant. Remove from pan and set aside.

2. In the same pan, heat olive oil over medium-high heat and add onion and garlic. Cook about 10–15 minutes, stirring occasionally, allowing onions to caramelize.

3. Place walnuts, onion-garlic mixture, lentils, soy sauce, and balsamic vinegar into a food processor. Process until mostly smooth, adding ½ cup water a few tablespoons at a time until mixture can process freely.

4. Serve on a plate with a drizzle of olive oil on top and an assortment of crackers.

HOT FUDGE SAUCE

» MAKES ABOUT 1 CUP «

½ cup vegan butter

½ cup sugar

¾ cup cocoa powder

⅔ cup soy creamer

1 teaspoon vanilla extract

When any old chocolate won't do, turn to this. It's equally delicious eaten warm and melty over a bowl of coconut ice cream or cold mixed into a soygurt smoothie. Get creative!

1. In a medium saucepan over medium-high heat, melt butter and add sugar, cocoa powder, and soy creamer, stirring constantly. Boil 1 minute.

2. Remove from heat and stir in vanilla. Sauce will thicken upon cooling and can be reheated.

3. Store in an airtight container in the refrigerator and use within 2 weeks.

PUMPKIN PIE DIP

Why be locked into an actual pie to enjoy pumpkin pie flavor? This way, you can eat the filling in whatever manner and with whichever vehicle you so desire—gingersnaps, graham crackers, pear slices, spoons, fingers...maybe it should be called Pumpkin Freedom Dip!

» MAKES 2 CUPS «

1 cup powdered sugar

2 (8-ounce) containers vegan cream cheese

1 (15-ounce) can pumpkin purée

1 teaspoon vanilla extract

1 teaspoon ground cinnamon

¼ teaspoon ground ginger

¼ teaspoon ground nutmeg

¼ teaspoon ground clove

1. With a mixer or by hand, beat powdered sugar into the cream cheese until smooth.

2. Stir in pumpkin, vanilla, cinnamon, ginger, nutmeg, and clove until completely mixed. Refrigerate overnight.

CARAMEL SAUCE

Think beyond ice cream with this buttery-sweet sauce. (It really begs to be paired with a big bowl of crisp, sliced apples.)

» MAKES ABOUT 1 CUP «

¼ cup sugar

¾ cup packed brown sugar

½ cup soy creamer

¼ cup vegan butter

1 teaspoon vanilla extract

1. In a medium saucepan over medium-high heat, stir sugar, brown sugar, creamer, and butter with a whisk.

2. Bring to a full boil and continue cooking, stirring constantly, 1 minute.

3. Remove from heat. Stir in vanilla. Sauce will thicken as it cools and can be reheated.

4. Store in an airtight container in the refrigerator and use within 2 weeks.

CHOCOLATE CHIP COOKIE DOUGH DIP

Because we all know the dough is the best part of chocolate chip cookies. Serve this dip with graham crackers.

« – »

1. In a stand mixer or by hand, beat cream cheese, butter, and coconut oil until fluffy.

2. Mix in powdered sugar, brown sugar, vanilla, salt, chocolate chips, and walnuts until combined.

1 (8-ounce) container vegan cream cheese

¼ cup vegan butter

¼ cup coconut oil, softened

1 cup powdered sugar

¼ cup brown sugar

1 teaspoon vanilla extract

½ teaspoon salt

1 cup vegan chocolate chips

1 cup chopped walnuts

CHAPTER 7

Savory Treats

With a Touch of Sugar and Spices

PRETZEL BARS

Salty, sweet, and crunchy! Consider yourself forewarned: These disappear fast.

» SERVES 6 «

1 cup brown sugar

½ cup vegan butter

1 teaspoon salt

1½ cups crushed pretzels

½ cup peanuts or almonds, chopped

¼ cup vegan chocolate chips

- -

1. Grease an 8" × 8" baking dish.

2. In a small saucepan over medium-high heat, bring brown sugar, butter, and salt to a boil. Boil 4 minutes. Remove from heat.

3. In a medium bowl, stir pretzels and peanuts together. Pour into brown sugar mixture.

4. Press into prepared baking dish.

5. While hot, press chocolate chips into the top and spread evenly after they melt. Let cool completely before cutting into squares.

CHEESY POPCORN

If you like popcorn, you'll love this even better. But don't bother making it if you don't have nutritional yeast—it's the magical ingredient that turns this cheesy.

» SERVES 4 «

2 tablespoons oil

½ cup corn kernels

½ cup nutritional yeast

1 teaspoon salt

½ teaspoon mustard powder

- -

1. In a large stockpot with a lid, heat oil over medium-high heat, with a few kernels of corn in it. When those kernels pop, remove pot from heat, pour in the rest of the corn, and put the lid on. Warming all the kernels ensures that most will pop.

2. Wait about 30 seconds. Return pot to heat and shake pan as kernels begin to pop. When the popping slows to just one or two pops, remove from heat.

3. In a large bowl, toss hot popcorn with nutritional yeast, salt, and mustard powder.

BAKED CURRIED SWEET POTATO FRIES

I adore sweet potatoes and eat them no fewer than four times a week, no joke. But I've never had a batch of sweet potato fries while eating out that meet my high expectations the way these do. The potatoes bake up soft inside, crisp outside, and you get a fragrant hint of curry. Man, are these good!

« – »

1. Preheat oven to 375°F. Line a baking sheet with lightly oiled parchment paper.

2. In a medium bowl, toss potatoes with olive oil, curry powder, salt, and coriander powder. Arrange in a single layer on prepared baking sheet.

3. Bake 35 minutes, turning halfway through cooking.

» SERVES 2 «

1 large sweet potato, peeled and cut into thin sticks

1 tablespoon olive oil

1 tablespoon curry powder, spicy or mild

1 teaspoon salt

½ teaspoon coriander powder

MEXICALI FONDUE

» SERVES 4–6 «

¾ cup Soyrizo (about 6 ounces)

1 medium red bell pepper, seeded and diced

1 tablespoon oil

3 tablespoons flour

2 cups nondairy milk

¼ cup nutritional yeast

2 cups vegan Cheddar shreds

Tortilla chips

Soyrizo is a vegan version of traditional chorizo, which is a spicy sausage that hails from Spain but is also very popular in Mexico. Several manufacturers offer Soyrizo, so shop around to see which has the spiciness you desire. If you can't stand the heat, you may want to steer clear of this dip.

« – »

1. Preheat oven to broil. Lightly grease a 1-quart baking dish.

2. In a medium sauté pan over medium-high heat, sauté Soyrizo and red pepper in oil. Cook until red pepper is tender, about 5 minutes.

3. Using a whisk, stir flour into Soyrizo mixture and cook 1 minute.

4. Add milk, stirring constantly until mixture boils and thickens. Add nutritional yeast and 1 cup vegan cheese.

5. Pour into prepared baking dish. Top with remaining cheese.

6. Place under broiler about 5 minutes or until top is golden.

7. Serve with tortilla chips.

CHEESY and SPICY ROASTED CHICKPEAS

» SERVES 4 «

1 (15-ounce) can garbanzo beans, drained and rinsed

1 tablespoon olive oil

¼ cup nutritional yeast

1 teaspoon chili powder

½ teaspoon cumin

Nutty, crunchy yumminess is what you have here. Better start buying garbanzo beans in bulk because these tasty snacks are truly addictive!

« – »

1. Preheat oven to 350°F. Line a baking sheet with parchment paper.

2. In a large bowl, toss together garbanzo beans, olive oil, nutritional yeast, chili powder, and cumin.

3. Pour out onto prepared baking sheet.

4. Bake 20–25 minutes, stirring about halfway through.

CHOCOLATE-COVERED POTATO CHIPS

The combo of crunchy potato chips plus melted chocolate yields a sinful result that belongs in the Junk Food Hall of Fame. (If only there were such a place...)

1 (12-ounce) bag vegan chocolate chips

1 teaspoon coconut oil

20 ruffled potato chips

Vegan sprinkles (optional)

½ cup shredded coconut (optional)

¼ cup pecans, chopped (optional)

1. Line a baking sheet with parchment paper.

2. In a small saucepan over medium heat, melt chocolate chips and coconut oil, stirring constantly, and remove from heat when most but not all chips are melted. Continue stirring until smooth.

3. Being careful not to break each potato chip, place one chip at a time in chocolate and, using two forks, turn chip in chocolate and lift, allowing excess chocolate to drip off. Place each chip on prepared baking sheet. Alternatively, dip only half of chip into chocolate. Dip in sprinkles, coconut, or pecans (if using) while chocolate is still melted.

4. Allow to cool on baking sheet until chocolate is set. Speed up process by refrigerating 5 minutes.

SWEET and SPICY NUT MIX

In the mood for something hot and sweet? In this recipe, wasabi peas and cayenne pepper provide the former, and brown sugar provides the latter. It's an unbeatable combo!

3 tablespoons packed brown sugar

1 tablespoon corn syrup

1 tablespoon vegan butter, melted

1 teaspoon salt

½ teaspoon ground cinnamon

¼ teaspoon cayenne pepper

1 cup raw nuts (almonds, peanuts, cashews, or any combination)

1 cup pretzels

½ cup wasabi peas

1. Preheat oven to 350°F. In a medium bowl, combine brown sugar, corn syrup, melted butter, salt, cinnamon, and cayenne pepper. Add in nuts, pretzels, and wasabi peas. Stir to evenly coat.

2. Place nut mixture evenly spread out on a cookie sheet.

3. Bake 10–15 minutes, stirring occasionally to break up clusters. Allow to cool completely.

EASY CANDIED ALMONDS

½ cup brown sugar

3 tablespoons vegan butter

½ teaspoon salt

1 cup raw almonds

Crunchy, sweet, nutty, and *fast*. You'll be chowing down in no time.

« - »

1. Line a cookie sheet with lightly greased foil.

2. In a small saucepan over medium-high heat, stir together brown sugar, butter, and salt until sugar melts. Stir in almonds. Bring to a boil and reduce heat to medium.

3. Cook until mixture is golden, about 5 minutes. Remove from heat.

4. Pour onto prepared cookie sheet and allow to cool. Break into bite-sized pieces.

CHEESY KALE CHIPS

» SERVES 4 «

1 bunch kale, rinsed and dried

2 tablespoons oil

1 teaspoon salt

½ cup nutritional yeast

⅛ teaspoon cayenne pepper

I'm sure you wouldn't believe me if I told you these kale chips actually have a flavor somewhat reminiscent of tortilla chips, so I think you should bake up a batch and see for yourself.

1. Preheat oven to 325°F. Line a baking sheet with parchment paper.

2. Remove stems and spines from kale and cut larger kale pieces in half.

3. In a large bowl, toss kale with oil, salt, nutritional yeast, and cayenne pepper, using hands to rub seasoning into leaves.

4. Place in a single layer on prepared baking sheet; you might cook this in batches, depending on the size of your bunch of kale.

5. Bake 20 minutes, turning halfway through. Kale should be crisp but not brown.

LAYERED PIZZA DIP

» SERVES 4–6 «

1 (8-ounce) container vegan cream cheese

1 (3-ounce) package sun-dried tomatoes, chopped

1 teaspoon oregano

1 cup marinara sauce

½ cup vegan pepperoni slices

¼ cup thinly sliced mushrooms

¼ cup thinly sliced bell peppers

¼ cup thinly sliced onions

1 cup vegan mozzarella shreds

1 French bread baguette

Perfect for when you can't be bothered with making dough for pizza, this warm, flavorful, multilayered dip (which feels more like a casserole) can be sopped up with big hunks of fresh French bread.

1. Preheat oven to 350°F. Lightly grease a 9" × 9" baking dish.

2. In a small bowl, mix cream cheese, sun-dried tomatoes, and oregano. Spread in the bottom of prepared dish. Top with marinara.

3. Layer pepperoni slices, mushrooms, bell peppers, and onions on marinara. Top with mozzarella cheese.

4. Bake 20–25 minutes or until vegetables are tender and mozzarella is melted.

5. Serve with French bread torn into pieces.

WHITE CHOCOLATE POTATO CHIP CLUSTERS

If there's any dark or milk chocolate around, I almost always go for that over the white variety. That is, except when white chocolate is melted and mixed with crushed chips and peanuts, as it is in this brilliant recipe.

» SERVES 4 «

3 cups plain potato chips, crushed

½ cup peanuts, chopped

1 cup vegan white chocolate chips

1. Line a cookie sheet with parchment paper.

2. In a medium bowl, toss together potato chips and peanuts.

3. In a small saucepan over medium heat, add white chocolate. Take chocolate off the heat while some chips are still melting and stir until smooth.

4. Pour melted chocolate over chips and nuts; toss with 2 spoons to coat evenly.

5. Drop by the heaping tablespoonful onto prepared cookie sheet. Cool completely before eating.

CARAMEL POPCORN

This honestly rivals the delicious stuff you can buy by the bucketload at the carnival. Perfect for the cravings that strike when the fair isn't in town.

1 cup sugar

½ cup corn syrup

½ cup water

2 tablespoons vegan butter

1 teaspoon vanilla extract

4 quarts popped popcorn

1. Line a cookie sheet with foil and lightly grease it. In a medium saucepan over medium-high heat, stir together sugar, corn syrup, and water. Bring to a rapid boil, turn heat down to medium, and allow to cook 10 minutes, watching for it to turn a golden color or to reach 300°F on a candy thermometer. Remove from heat.

2. Stir in butter and vanilla; pour over popcorn and toss with 2 wooden spoons to coat evenly.

3. Place popcorn on prepared cookie sheet to cool.

CHAPTER 8

Cakewalk (Pies, Too)

Who Needs Butter?

RICH CHOCOLATE CAKE *with* CHOCOLATE GANACHE

If chocolate is your vice of choice, this cake will become a kitchen staple. It's moist, rich, and überchocolaty.

» SERVES 10–12 «

2 cups soy milk

1 tablespoon apple cider vinegar

1¾ cups sugar

⅔ cup vegetable oil

1½ teaspoons vanilla extract

2 cups flour

⅔ cup cocoa powder

1½ teaspoons baking soda

1 teaspoon baking powder

½ teaspoon salt

1. Preheat oven to 350°F. Grease and flour two 9" round cake pans.

2. In a small bowl, add soy milk and vinegar; set aside 5 minutes to thicken.

3. In a large bowl or mixer, stir together sugar, oil, and vanilla.

4. In a medium bowl, sift together flour, cocoa powder, baking soda, baking powder, and salt. If you do not have a sifter, a whisk works well to combine the dry ingredients.

5. Add dry ingredients to wet ingredients and stir by hand until very smooth or for 2 minutes using a mixer.

6. Divide batter evenly between prepared cake pans. Bake 25 minutes or until a toothpick comes out mostly clean, checking often toward the end; do not overbake.

7. Allow to cool, then invert one cake layer onto a cake plate. Pour Chocolate Ganache over bottom layer, top with second layer, and pour ganache over the top, allowing it to pour down the sides of the cake. Refrigerate cake to allow ganache to set up.

Chocolate Ganache

½ cup soy milk

12 ounces vegan chocolate chips

2 tablespoons vegan butter or coconut oil

1. Scald (bring to a boil) soy milk, remove from heat, add chocolate chips and butter or oil, and stir until smooth.

2. Remove from heat. Allow to cool slightly.

BOSTON CREAM PIE

» SERVES 8–10 «

1 cup soy milk

1 tablespoon apple cider
vinegar

2 cups self-rising flour

1 teaspoon baking soda

1 cup sugar

¼ cup applesauce

½ cup oil

1 teaspoon vanilla extract

Need proof that nearly anything can be veganized?
Here's how to re-create the original Boston Cream Pie
with dense sponge cake, a light and creamy whipped
vanilla custard, and decadent chocolate ganache.

1. Preheat oven to 350°F. Grease and flour two round 8" cake
pans.

2. In a small bowl, combine soy milk and vinegar; set aside
5 minutes.

3. In a medium bowl, sift flour and baking soda.

4. In a medium bowl, mix together sugar, applesauce, oil, and
vanilla. Stir in soy milk mixture. Add to dry ingredients and mix
well until smooth. Pour into prepared cake pans.

5. Bake 25 minutes. Cool in pan.

(continued on next page ▶)

Custard Filling

1. In a small bowl, whisk together 2 cups soy milk and custard powder, then pour into a medium saucepan over medium heat. Bring to a boil, stirring constantly, and cook until custard mixture is very thick, about 5 minutes. When mixture becomes very stiff, remove from heat. Cool completely before next step.

2. In a stand mixer, beat butter, sugar, and vanilla until very light and fluffy, about 5 minutes on high.

3. Add custard mixture and remaining 2 tablespoons soy milk to the beaten butter and continue beating until they are completely incorporated and thick.

4. Place bottom layer of cake onto a cake plate. Spoon on custard. Top with second layer of cake.

> **2 cups plus 2 tablespoons soy milk, divided**
>
> **¼ cup custard powder**
>
> **1 cup vegan butter**
>
> **1 cup sugar**
>
> **1 teaspoon vanilla extract**

Chocolate Ganache

1. Scald (bring to a boil) soy milk, remove from heat, add chocolate chips and butter or oil, and stir until smooth.

2. Remove from heat. Allow to cool slightly.

3. Pour over cake when thick but still liquid. Refrigerate cake to allow ganache to set up and to keep custard firm.

> **½ cup soy milk**
>
> **12 ounces vegan chocolate chips**
>
> **2 tablespoons vegan butter or coconut oil**

CHOCOLATE MINT COOKIE LAYER CAKE

1 recipe Rich Chocolate Cake
(see recipe in this chapter)

1 cup vegan butter

4 cups powdered sugar

½ teaspoon mint extract

2 tablespoons nondairy milk

20 Oreo cookies, 15 of them
crushed

For when Girl Scouts Thin Mints are just not in season, stock your pantry with this layer cake, and you can enjoy the same awesome combo of chocolate and mint. The middle layer has a crunchy surprise brought on by the addition of Oreo cookies! (Yep, they're vegan.)

1. Bake Rich Chocolate Cake as directed. Allow to cool.

2. To make frosting, beat butter in a stand mixer or by hand until light and fluffy. Stir in powdered sugar, mint extract, and milk, and continue to beat 4 minutes.

3. Spoon ⅓ of frosting into a medium bowl and fold in crushed cookies.

4. Place one layer of cake on a cake plate. Top with cookie-frosting mixture and spread evenly. Top with second layer of cake; use remaining frosting to cover top and sides of cake.

Mint Drizzle

½ cup vegan chocolate chips

½ teaspoon mint extract

1. In a small saucepan over low heat, melt chocolate chips, stirring constantly, until most are melted. Remove from heat and stir until smooth. Stir in mint extract. Allow to cool slightly.

2. Drizzle chocolate over cake, making a crosshatch pattern on top and letting chocolate drip down sides.

3. Top cake with remaining 5 Oreo cookies cut in half and placed on the cut end.

S'MORES CAKE *with* MARSHMALLOW FROSTING

We could also call this the "Campfire Cake," it so closely emulates the flavor and texture of the classic camping dessert. Make sure to seek out vegan marshmallow cream; traditional marshmallow contains gelatin—no good.

« - »

1. In a small saucepan over low heat, melt chocolate chips, stirring constantly, and remove from heat when most chips are melted. Stir until smooth.

2. Line a cookie sheet with parchment paper. Scatter graham cracker pieces in a single layer. Pour melted chocolate over graham pieces, tossing to coat evenly. Refrigerate to set chocolate.

3. In a stand mixer or by hand, beat butter until light and fluffy. Stir in powdered sugar and milk and continue to beat 4 minutes.

4. With a wooden spoon, fold in Ricemellow Creme gently.

5. Place one layer of cake on a cake plate. Add about ⅓ of the frosting and spread evenly. Top with second layer of cake; use remaining frosting to cover top and sides of cake.

6. Remove chocolate-covered graham crackers from refrigerator and break up into bite-sized chunks. Pile them on top of cake. Keep refrigerated.

>> **SERVES 10–12** «

1 cup vegan semisweet chocolate chips

2 cups graham crackers, crushed into ½" pieces

1 cup vegan butter

4 cups powdered sugar

2 tablespoons nondairy milk

1 (10-ounce) container Suzanne's Specialties Ricemellow Creme vegan marshmallow cream

1 recipe Rich Chocolate Cake, baked in 2 (9") round cake pans (see recipe in this chapter)

BANANA CHOCOLATE CHIP CUPCAKES
with GANACHE

A fun and chocolaty twist on banana bread! And a great way to use up overripe fruit—the bananas mash into the batter a whole lot easier.

«- -»

1. Preheat oven to 350°F. Line a 12-cup muffin tin with paper liners or grease and flour well.

2. In a medium bowl, stir together sugar, oil, mashed bananas, milk, and vanilla.

3. In separate medium bowl, sift together flour, baking soda, and salt. Add to banana mixture and mix until smooth. Stir in chocolate chips.

4. Fill prepared muffin cups ¾ full.

5. Bake 15–17 minutes or until cupcakes are golden and center springs back when lightly touched. Cool completely.

6. Place a banana slice on top of each cupcake; pour a heaping teaspoonful of ganache over banana. Let ganache set.

» **MAKES 12 CUPCAKES** «

1 cup sugar

½ cup oil

4 medium ripe bananas, mashed

¼ cup nondairy milk

1 teaspoon vanilla extract

2 cups flour

1 teaspoon baking soda

1 teaspoon salt

1 cup vegan chocolate chips

1 medium banana, sliced

1 recipe Chocolate Ganache (see recipe in this chapter)

ROOT BEER FLOAT CUPCAKES

» MAKES 12 CUPCAKES «

1 (12-ounce) can root beer plus 1 cup root beer

2 tablespoons ground flaxseeds

¼ cup water

1 cup vegan butter

1½ cups sugar

2½ cups flour

2 teaspoons baking powder

1 teaspoon salt

Why settle for grabbing a soda when you can have root beer in the form of a cake? Watch out: too much root beer reduction may send you to the dentist!

1. In a medium saucepan over high heat, bring 1 can of root beer to a boil. Reduce heat to medium and simmer, stirring occasionally. Root beer should reduce down until only about 25 percent of liquid is left or until root beer reduction coats the back of a spoon, 25–30 minutes. Cool completely before using.

2. Preheat oven to 350°F. Line a 12-cup cupcake tin with paper liners.

3. In a small bowl, mix flaxseeds and water; set aside.

4. In a mixer, cream butter and sugar until light and fluffy. Add 1 cup root beer and 1 tablespoon root beer reduction and mix well.

5. In a medium bowl, mix together flour, baking powder, and salt. Add to creamed butter and mix until smooth.

6. Fill prepared cupcake tins ¾ full. Bake 18 minutes. Cool completely.

7. Frost with Root Beer Frosting and drizzle extra root beer reduction on top.

Root Beer Frosting

1 cup vegan butter

4 cups powdered sugar

2 tablespoons root beer reduction

Beat butter until light and fluffy; add powdered sugar and root beer reduction. Continue to beat until very fluffy.

BLACK FOREST CUPCAKES

Rich and tart, these decadent treats deserve top billing in the vast world of vegan cupcakes. They feature a dense cake, a hint of brandy, fluffy white frosting, and a brilliant crown of cherries.

» MAKES 12 CUPCAKES «

1 recipe Rich Chocolate Cake (see recipe in this chapter)

1 (15-ounce) can pitted sour cherries, drained, liquid reserved

½ cup sugar

2 tablespoons cornstarch

¼ teaspoon almond extract (or ½ teaspoon vanilla extract)

½ cup nonhydrogenated vegetable shortening

5 cups powdered sugar

1–2 tablespoons nondairy milk

1 teaspoon vanilla extract

4 tablespoons kirsch brandy

1. Preheat oven to 350°F. Line a 12-cup muffin tin with paper liners or grease and flour well. Fill prepared muffin cups ¾ full with Rich Chocolate Cake recipe.

2. Bake 15–17 minutes or until inserted toothpick comes out mostly clean and centers spring back when lightly touched. Cool completely.

3. In a small bowl, whisk together ½ cup reserved cherry liquid, sugar, and cornstarch until cornstarch is dissolved.

4. In a medium saucepan over medium-high heat, stir cornstarch mixture until it comes to a boil and thickens. Stir in cherries and bring back to a simmer. Cook 3 minutes longer. Remove from heat and stir in ¼ teaspoon almond extract. Allow to cool.

5. In a stand mixer or by hand, beat shortening until very fluffy. Add in powdered sugar and 1 tablespoon milk. Beat until light and fluffy, adding last tablespoon of milk if frosting is too stiff. Add 1 teaspoon vanilla extract.

6. Brush tops of cupcakes with kirsch, frost each with a heaping tablespoonful of frosting, and add a teaspoonful of the cherry mixture.

WHITE CHOCOLATE RASPBERRY CHEESECAKE

» SERVES 10–12 «

15 Oreo cookies, finely crushed

4 tablespoons vegan butter, softened

1 (16-ounce) package firm tofu, drained

2 (8-ounce) containers vegan cream cheese

¾ cup sugar

¼ cup oil

2 tablespoons lemon juice

½ teaspoon salt

1 teaspoon vanilla extract

1 cup vegan white chocolate chips, divided

¼ cup raspberry jam

Your palate will feel like it's taken a trip to paradise after you bite into this awesome creation, courtesy of crushed Oreo cookies, white chocolate, and a swirl of raspberry jam.

« – »

1. Preheat oven to 350°F. Lightly grease a 9" springform pan.

2. In a small bowl, mix cookie crumbs with butter. Press into prepared pan.

3. In a blender, add tofu, cream cheese, sugar, oil, lemon juice, salt, and vanilla. Blend until very smooth, about 2 minutes.

4. In a small microwave-safe container, melt ½ cup white chocolate chips, cooking at 15-second intervals, stirring after each interval until chocolate is smooth.

5. In a large bowl, stir together blended ingredients, melted white chocolate, and remaining ½ cup white chocolate chips.

6. Pour over cookie crust, reserving ½ cup batter.

7. In a small bowl, mix reserved batter with raspberry jam.

8. Spoon raspberry batter on top of cheesecake in a random pattern. Using a butter knife, swirl lightly to marble top of cheesecake.

9. Bake 45 minutes. Turn oven off, leaving cheesecake in oven without opening door for another 20 minutes. Remove from oven and cool on counter. Refrigerate overnight.

PIÑA COLADA CHEESECAKE

» SERVES 10–12 «

1½ cups pineapple juice, divided

2 tablespoons cornstarch

1½ cups graham cracker crumbs

2 tablespoons sugar

4 tablespoons vegan butter

8 ounces firm tofu

4 (8-ounce) containers vegan cream cheese

1½ cups (12 ounces) piña colada mixer

2 tablespoons coconut rum

Tofu adds structure to lots of vegan cheesecakes, and this coconut rum and pineapple-flavored variety is no exception. Indulge when you're feeling like a taste of the tropical.

» – «

1. Preheat oven to 350°F. Lightly grease a 9" springform pan.

2. In a small saucepan over medium-high heat, bring 1¼ cups pineapple juice to a boil. Cook about 10 minutes or until juice reduces by half.

3. In a small bowl, stir cornstarch into remaining ¼ cup pineapple juice and then add to saucepan, stirring constantly until very thick, about 3–5 minutes. Remove from heat.

4. In a separate small bowl, mix graham cracker crumbs and sugar with butter. Press into prepared pan.

5. To a blender, add tofu, cream cheese, piña colada mix, and rum and blend until very smooth, about 2 minutes.

6. Pour over graham cracker crust, reserving ½ cup batter.

7. In a small bowl, mix together thickened pineapple juice and reserved batter.

8. Spoon pineapple batter on top of cheesecake in a random pattern. Using a butter knife, swirl lightly to marble top of cheesecake.

9. Bake 45 minutes. Turn oven off, leaving cheesecake in oven without opening door for another 20 minutes.

10. Remove from oven and cool on counter. Refrigerate overnight.

LEMONY BLUEBERRY CRISP

This comes together in a snap and cooks into a thickened pie with lots of lemony flavor and a crispy crunchy top. Try it alongside vegan ice cream.

» SERVES 6 «

1. Preheat oven to 350°F. Have ready a 9" × 13" baking dish.

2. In a large bowl, toss together blueberries, tapioca, sugar, and lemon zest. Pour into baking dish.

3. In a medium bowl, combine oats, bread crumbs, butter, brown sugar, and almonds until butter is incorporated and mixture is crumbly. Pour over blueberries.

4. Bake 45 minutes or until crumbs are golden brown. Serve hot or cold.

5 cups fresh blueberries

2 teaspoons instant tapioca

2 tablespoons sugar

Zest of 2 medium lemons

1 cup quick oats

1 cup plain bread crumbs

½ cup vegan butter

½ cup brown sugar

½ cup slivered almonds

PEACH SCHNAPPS COBBLER

When you're craving something with warm flavors— nutmeg, cinnamon, and a buttery crust—this is your go-to. When right out of the oven, pour soy creamer on top and gobble up (before you're forced to share!).

» SERVES 6 «

1. Preheat oven to 350°F. Put butter in a 9" × 13" baking dish and place in the oven.

2. In a small bowl, mix milk and vinegar; set aside 5 minutes.

3. In a medium bowl, sift flour, 1 cup sugar, baking powder, and salt. Stir in milk/vinegar mix and schnapps.

4. In another medium bowl, mix together peaches, remaining sugar, tapioca, cinnamon, and nutmeg.

5. Pour batter over hot butter and follow with peach mixture.

6. Bake 25–30 minutes or until cake is golden and has pulled away from sides of pan. Serve warm.

1 cup vegan butter

1 cup nondairy milk

1 tablespoon vinegar

1 cup flour

1¼ cups sugar, divided

1 teaspoon baking powder

½ teaspoon salt

2 tablespoons peach schnapps

5 cups peeled, pitted, and sliced peaches (roughly 2 pounds)

1 tablespoon instant tapioca

½ teaspoon ground cinnamon

¼ teaspoon ground nutmeg

CHOCOLATE PEANUT BUTTER PUDDING PIE *with* PRETZEL CRUST

1½ cups crushed pretzels

3 tablespoons sugar

½ cup vegan butter, melted

2 cups vegan chocolate chips

2 cups nondairy milk

3 tablespoons cornstarch

¼ cup coconut oil

½ cup peanut butter

1 teaspoon salt

⅓ cup sugar

If you like Reese's peanut butter cups, this vegan alternative is even better! This dense pie features a crunchy pretzel crust sure to satisfy your fiercest salty-sweet craving.

1. Preheat oven to 350°F.

2. In a small bowl, mix together crushed pretzels, sugar, and butter. Press into a 9" pie pan.

3. Bake crust 8–10 minutes.

4. Place chocolate chips into a large bowl.

5. In a medium saucepan off the heat, whisk together milk and cornstarch. Turn heat to medium; add coconut oil, peanut butter, salt, and sugar. Stirring constantly, bring to a boil and allow to cook until very thick. Remove from heat.

6. Pour mixture over chocolate chips and stir until chips are melted and filling is smooth.

7. Spoon into prepared crust and refrigerate 2 hours.

TAPIOCA RUM CUSTARD

You could also use instant tapioca for this, but it's a lot pricier than buying the tapioca pearls. If you use the pearls, don't skip the soaking step, or you'll have a crunchy custard. This tastes great warm or cold!

-- -- -- -- -- -- -- -- -- -- -- -- -- -- -- -- -- -- --

1. In a small bowl, soak tapioca pearls in milk at least 1 hour. Overnight is best.

2. In a medium saucepan, whisk together soaked pearls and milk with cornstarch and sugar.

3. Turn heat to medium-high and bring to a boil, stirring occasionally. Turn down to medium-low and let cook 20 minutes, stirring often.

4. Taste for doneness. Tapioca pearls should be translucent and soft. Remove from heat.

5. Stir in vanilla and rum. Cover with plastic and let sit on the counter 10 minutes.

>> SERVES 4 <<

⅓ cup small tapioca pearls
2 cups nondairy milk
2 tablespoons cornstarch
⅓ cup sugar
1 teaspoon vanilla extract
2 tablespoons rum

GOLDEN MILK CUSTARD

Golden milk is a yellow and richly spiced drink that lends itself well to this creamy custard dessert.

-- -- -- -- -- -- -- -- -- -- -- -- -- -- -- -- -- -- --

1. In a medium saucepan off the heat, whisk together cornstarch and coconut milk until smooth. Add sugar and spices, turn heat to medium-high, and bring to a full boil, stirring constantly. Cook until mixture thickens, about 5 minutes. Remove from heat. Stir in vanilla.

2. Spoon pudding into 4 small bowls and refrigerate 4 hours or until completely cool.

>> SERVES 4 <<

½ cup cornstarch
2½ cups coconut milk
½ cup sugar
1 teaspoon ground turmeric
1 teaspoon ground cinnamon
½ teaspoon ginger powder
Small pinch of black pepper
1 teaspoon vanilla extract

COCONUT CRÈME BRÛLÉE

» SERVES 4 «

½ cup cornstarch

2½ cups coconut milk

½ cup plus 2 tablespoons sugar, divided

1 teaspoon vanilla extract

2 tablespoons coconut flakes

This is like traditional crème brûlée, but it's much more delicious with the addition of coconut—a vegan favorite that also happens to be healthy. Of course, here we corrupt it with copious amounts of sugar!

1. Preheat oven to broil. Lightly grease four ramekins.

2. In a medium saucepan off the heat, whisk together cornstarch and coconut milk until smooth. Add ½ cup sugar and turn heat to medium-high; bring to a full boil, stirring constantly. Cook until mixture thickens, about 5 minutes. Remove from heat. Stir in vanilla and coconut flakes.

3. Fill prepared ramekins and sprinkle remaining sugar on top of each.

4. Place under broiler. Cook until sugar melts and begins to turn a light caramel color.

BLUEBERRY POUND CAKE

This recipe was made for blueberry season, but any fruit that's not afraid of the oven can flavor this buttery cake. Try apricots or other fresh berries.

½ cup vegan butter

½ cup sugar

6 ounces firm tofu

½ cup water

2 teaspoons vanilla extract

2 cups cake flour

2 teaspoons baking powder

1½ cups fresh blueberries

«‐ »

1. Preheat oven to 350°F. Line a 9" × 5" loaf pan with parchment paper.

2. In a mixer, cream butter and sugar on high speed.

3. In a high-speed blender, purée tofu and water until very smooth. Add to butter mixture with vanilla and mix until well combined.

4. In a medium bowl, sift together flour and baking powder. Add flour mixture to ingredients in mixer in two batches; beat together 1 minute. Fold in blueberries.

5. Bake 55 minutes or until a toothpick comes out clean. Allow to cool completely in pan before cutting.

SWEET PIE CRUST

This flaky crust for fruit or custard pies should move into your vegan baking recipe box, as you'll use it time and again to make your favorite junk food. Homemade always beats store-bought when it comes to crusts.

3 cups flour

2 teaspoons sugar

1 teaspoon salt

1½ cups Spectrum nonhydrogenated vegetable shortening, chilled

⅓ cup ice water

«‐ »

1. In a food processor with the blade fitting attached, pulse flour, sugar, salt, and shortening until mixture resembles coarse meal. Alternatively, used a pastry blender or two knives to cut shortening into flour.

2. Add water 1 tablespoon at a time until a spoonful of dough can be shaped into a ball that doesn't fall apart; do not overmix.

3. Divide dough in half, shape each half into a ball, and flatten into a disk. Wrap in plastic and refrigerate at least 1 hour.

GLAZED ORANGE LOAF

» SERVES 8 «

1 cup soy milk

Juice of 1 medium orange, divided

2 cups flour

½ teaspoon baking powder

½ teaspoon baking soda

½ teaspoon salt

1 cup sugar

⅓ cup vegetable oil

½ teaspoon vanilla extract

1 tablespoon orange zest

1 cup powdered sugar

There's lots of citrus bursting from this sticky glazed loaf, a perfect dessert after breakfast or dinner.

1. Preheat oven to 350°F. Line a 9" × 5" loaf pan with parchment paper.

2. In a large bowl, combine soy milk and ½ of orange juice, set aside.

3. In a medium bowl, sift together flour, baking powder, baking soda, and salt.

4. To milk mixture, add sugar, oil, vanilla, and zest. Stir to combine. Add flour mixture half at a time to milk mixture, mixing to combine well, but don't overmix.

5. Bake 40 minutes or until a toothpick comes out clean.

6. In a small bowl, mix remaining orange juice with powdered sugar and pour over loaf hot from the oven. Allow to cool completely before cutting.

PUMPKIN GINGERSNAP ICE CREAM PIE

» SERVES 6–8 «

30 vegan gingersnaps

2 cups pumpkin purée

1 cup sugar

1 teaspoon salt

2 teaspoons pumpkin pie spice

1 cup pecans, chopped

1 pint vegan vanilla ice cream, softened

Warming flavors in a cooling format—serve this when you want to surprise your guests with the contrast of flavors and textures.

1. Line a 9" springform pan with about 10 gingersnaps.

2. In a large bowl, mix pumpkin, sugar, salt, pumpkin pie spice, pecans, and ice cream.

3. Spoon half of pumpkin mixture over gingersnaps. Add 10 more gingersnaps over pumpkin layer. Top with remaining pumpkin mixture. Crush remaining gingersnaps and press into top of pie.

4. Freeze at least 3 hours before serving.

PUMPKIN PIE *with* BOURBON PRALINE SAUCE

For when you can't decide between pumpkin and pecan pie, here's the best of both worlds. Not in the mood to make pie? Make the Bourbon Praline Sauce instead and pour over a scoop of vegan vanilla ice cream for an equally exciting dessert.

« – »

>> SERVES 6–8 <<

½ recipe Sweet Pie Crust (see recipe in this chapter)

1 (16-ounce) package silken tofu

1 (16-ounce) can pure pumpkin

⅔ cup sugar

2 teaspoons pumpkin pie spice

1 tablespoon bourbon

1. Preheat oven to 425°F. Roll crust out to fit into a 9" pie pan, trim any overhang, and crimp edges with a fork. Place on a cookie sheet.

2. In a food processor, blend tofu until very smooth. Add pumpkin, sugar, pumpkin pie spice, and bourbon. Process until very smooth.

3. Pour into prepared pie crust.

4. Bake 10 minutes. Lower oven temperature to 350°F and bake 45 more minutes.

5. Cool completely. Refrigerate a few hours or overnight before cutting. Pour warm Bourbon Praline Sauce over the top before serving.

Bourbon Praline Sauce

1. In a medium saucepan over medium-high heat, stir together butter, soy creamer, and brown sugar. Bring to a boil and let cook until it thickens, stirring constantly, about 5 minutes. Remove from heat.

2. Stir in bourbon and pecans. Serve warm over the pumpkin pie.

½ cup vegan butter

½ cup vegan soy creamer

1 cup brown sugar

¼ cup bourbon

1 cup pecans, chopped

PUMPKIN APPLE CAKE *with* GINGER FROSTING

2 medium baking apples, cored and sliced thinly

2 teaspoons ground cinnamon, divided

1 cup plus 1 tablespoon sugar, divided

1 cup vegan butter

1 cup applesauce

1 teaspoon vanilla extract

1 (15-ounce) can pure pumpkin

2 cups flour

1 teaspoon baking soda

1 teaspoon ground clove

1 teaspoon ground ginger

1 teaspoon salt

2 cups old-fashioned oats

FROSTING

½ cup nonhydrogenated vegetable shortening

4 cups powdered sugar

1 teaspoon ground ginger

½ teaspoon cardamom

½ teaspoon ground clove

2 tablespoons nondairy milk

You're in store for layers and layers of warm, spicy goodness when you craft this cake. Apply the icing straightaway once the cake comes from the oven so that you get a lovely, gooey ginger glaze once it cools. Now that you know the trick, get baking!

« – »

1. Preheat oven to 350°F. Lightly grease a 9" × 13" baking dish.

2. In a large bowl, toss apples with 1 teaspoon cinnamon and 1 tablespoon sugar. Line prepared baking dish with apples.

3. In a stand mixer or by hand, beat butter and 1 cup sugar until light and fluffy. Add applesauce, vanilla, and pumpkin, and mix to combine.

4. In a medium bowl, sift together flour, baking soda, remaining teaspoon cinnamon, clove, ginger, and salt. Add to pumpkin mixture and stir well, about 2 minutes. Stir in oats. Pour over apples in dish. Smooth top with a spatula.

5. Bake 35–40 minutes or until top springs back when lightly depressed.

6. While cake is baking, prepare frosting. In a stand mixer or by hand, cream shortening until light and fluffy, then add powdered sugar, ginger, cardamom, clove, and milk. Beat until all ingredients are combined. Spoon over top of cake as soon as it comes out of the oven.

7. Allow cake to cool about 15 minutes. Serve warm.

FROZEN LEMON CREAM PIE

Sweet, tart, creamy, cool, and delicious! Any recipe that includes sweetened condensed milk automatically qualifies as junk food of the most delicious degree.

» SERVES 6–8 «

« – »

1½ cups graham cracker crumbs

¼ cup sugar

4 tablespoons vegan butter, melted

2 (8-ounce) containers vegan cream cheese

1¾ cups vegan Sweetened Condensed Milk (see this page)

Zest and juice of 2 medium lemons (zest lemons before you squeeze them)

1. In a medium bowl, mix graham cracker crumbs, sugar, and butter. Press into a 9" pie pan, covering bottom and sides.

2. In a mixer, beat cream cheese until fluffy, then add Sweetened Condensed Milk, lemon zest, and lemon juice, and mix thoroughly.

3. Pour over crust and freeze 2 hours. If pie has been in the freezer overnight, let it thaw slightly before eating.

Sweetened Condensed Milk

4 cups soy milk

½ cup vegan butter

2 cups sugar

1 teaspoon salt

1. In a small saucepan, scald the soy milk; bring to a boil, turn heat down, and let simmer.

2. In a medium saucepan over medium-high heat, melt butter and add sugar and salt, stirring until sugar is melted.

3. Add the milk to the butter, slowly stirring constantly. Note the level of liquid in the pot; cook until it is reduced by half and the condensed milk is thick, about 5 minutes. Cool completely before using. (Makes about 2 cups.)

BERRY, PEACH, or PUMPKIN HAND PIES

» MAKES 1 DOZEN
MINI PIES «

1 recipe Sweet Pie Crust (see recipe in this chapter)

2 tablespoons nondairy milk

2 tablespoons raw sugar

Serve these sweet little pies to kids or when you want to wow with presentation. Use fresh fruit to make the creations that much more special.

« – »

1. Preheat oven to 350°F. Line a cookie sheet with parchment paper.

2. Roll out pie crust one disk at a time, rolling into a large rectangle about ⅛" thick. With a knife or pizza cutter, square edges of dough, then cut into 3" × 4" rectangles.

3. Prepare one or more of the Berry, Peach, or Pumpkin fillings.

4. Place a heaping tablespoonful of filling in the center of one dough rectangle, wet edge of dough, cover with a second rectangle, and crimp edges of dough closed with a fork.

5. Place on prepared cookie sheet. Brush with milk and sprinkle with raw sugar.

6. Bake 15–20 minutes or until edges are golden brown.

(continued on next page ▶)

Berry Filling

1. In a medium saucepan over medium heat, bring berries and sugar to a simmer; cook until sugar is melted, about 5 minutes.

2. Turn heat up to medium-high.

3. Combine cornstarch and water; add to saucepan.

4. Cook until it comes to a full boil and filling is clear and thick. Remove from heat.

> **2 cups ripe berries (blueberry, blackberry, or raspberry)**
>
> **½ cup sugar**
>
> **2 tablespoons cornstarch**
>
> **2 tablespoons water**

Peach Filling

1. In a medium saucepan over high heat, combine peaches, sugar, flour, cinnamon, nutmeg, lemon zest, and lemon juice, stirring constantly until mixture comes to a boil.

2. Turn heat to medium and simmer until mixture becomes thick, about 5 minutes.

3. Remove from heat.

> **2 cups peeled, pitted, and chopped peaches**
>
> **½ cup sugar**
>
> **2 tablespoons flour**
>
> **½ teaspoon ground cinnamon**
>
> **¼ teaspoon ground nutmeg**
>
> **1 teaspoon lemon zest**
>
> **1 teaspoon lemon juice**

Pumpkin Filling

1. In a medium saucepan over medium-high heat, combine pumpkin, brown sugar, cornstarch, salt, and pumpkin pie spice, whisking quickly to incorporate cornstarch.

2. Bring to a boil and cook until very thick, about 5 minutes.

3. Remove from heat.

> **2 cups canned pure pumpkin**
>
> **½ cup brown sugar**
>
> **4 tablespoons cornstarch**
>
> **1 teaspoon salt**
>
> **1½ teaspoons pumpkin pie spice**

DEEP-DISH APPLE BROWN SUGAR PIE

The brown sugar in this pie gives it a distinctly caramel flavor, perfect served with a dollop of coconut whipped topping or a scoop of vegan ice cream.

« – »

1. Preheat oven to 450°F. Roll out one disk of pie crust to fit a 9" deep-dish pie pan. Roll out second disk large enough to cover pie.

2. In a large bowl, combine apples, ¼ cup sugar, brown sugar, butter, flour, cinnamon, and nutmeg; mix well.

3. Spoon apple mixture into prepared crust. Top with pie dough, cut any excess, and crimp edge with a fork. Slice 4 (1") holes to vent pie. Brush with milk and sprinkle with 1 tablespoon sugar.

4. Bake 10 minutes. Turn oven down to 350°F and bake an additional 45 minutes. Cool completely before cutting.

» SERVES 6–8 «

1 recipe Sweet Pie Crust (see recipe in this chapter)

4 medium Granny Smith apples, peeled, cored, and sliced

¼ cup plus 1 tablespoon sugar, divided

1 cup brown sugar

2 tablespoons vegan butter, softened

3 tablespoons flour

1 teaspoon ground cinnamon

¼ teaspoon ground nutmeg

2 tablespoons nondairy milk

COCONUT CRUST BANANA CUSTARD PIE

1½ cups plus 2 tablespoons coconut, toasted, divided

½ cup graham cracker crumbs

1 cup plus 2 tablespoons sugar, divided

3 tablespoons vegan butter, melted

1 cup plus 2 tablespoons soy milk, divided

¼ cup custard powder

1 cup vegan butter

1 teaspoon vanilla extract

3 ripe medium bananas

Reminiscent of diner banana cream pie, but with the addition of coconut! Custard powder could be a tough ingredient to find; try a grocery that carries imported foods. You could try substituting cornstarch for the powder if you're really stuck.

1. Preheat oven to 350°F. Have ready a 9" pie plate.

2. In a medium bowl, combine 1½ cups coconut, graham cracker crumbs, 2 tablespoons sugar, and melted butter; mix until well combined. Press into pie plate, covering bottom and sides.

3. Bake 10 minutes. Cool.

4. In a small bowl, whisk together 1 cup soy milk and custard powder. Pour into a medium saucepan over medium heat. Bring to a boil, stirring constantly, and cook until mixture is very thick, about 5 minutes. Cool completely before next step.

5. In a stand mixer, beat 1 cup butter, 1 cup sugar, and vanilla until very light and fluffy, about 5 minutes on high.

6. Add custard mixture and 2 tablespoons soy milk to beaten butter mixture and continue beating until they are completely incorporated and thick and smooth.

7. Slice bananas into bottom of prepared crust. Spoon custard over bananas and refrigerate overnight. Top with Coconut Whipped Cream right before you serve and sprinkle with 2 tablespoons coconut.

Coconut Whipped Cream

1 (14-ounce) can coconut milk (not lite)

2 tablespoons powdered sugar

1 tablespoon cornstarch

1. Refrigerate can of coconut milk overnight or put in freezer 2 hours.

2. Open can and spoon out coconut milk solids, leaving liquid behind in can.

3. In a stand mixer or by hand, whip coconut solids, powdered sugar, and cornstarch 5 minutes until fluffy.

CHAPTER 9

Candy and Cookie Fix

For the Ultimate Sweet Tooth

CHOCOLATE PEANUT BUTTER WAFER CANDY BAR

» MAKES 24 BARS «

1 cup peanut butter

½ cup powdered sugar

¼ teaspoon salt

1 (14.1-ounce) package vanilla wafer cookies*

1 (12-ounce) package vegan chocolate chips

1 teaspoon vegan butter

*NOTE: Gefen wafers are vegan and can be found in the kosher section of your local grocery store or through online sources.

Did you know it's incredibly easy to make candy bars? You can become master of your junk food kingdom when you create these ridiculously cravable bars that are made up of a crispy wafer and sweet peanut butter, smothered in a chocolate outer layer.

« – »

1. In a medium bowl, combine peanut butter, powdered sugar, and salt. Press a heaping teaspoonful on top of each wafer.

2. Place chocolate chips and butter in a medium microwavable bowl. Microwave in 15-second intervals, stirring after each interval until chocolate is melted through.

3. Working with two forks, dip each peanut butter–topped wafer into the melted chocolate and turn to coat. Place on wax paper until chocolate is set.

ENGLISH TOFFEE

Buttery and crunchy—and better than the Brits can make!

» MAKES 1½ POUNDS «

1 cup sugar

1 cup vegan butter

1 cup almonds, chopped

3 teaspoons water

1 teaspoon vanilla extract

1 cup vegan semisweet chocolate chips

1. Lightly grease an 11" × 7" × 2" baking dish.

2. In a medium saucepan over medium-high heat, bring sugar, butter, 1 tablespoon almonds, and water to a boil, stirring constantly. Cook until a deep caramel color, about 15–20 minutes. Remove from heat, add vanilla, and pour into prepared baking dish.

3. Sprinkle chocolate chips over toffee and spread evenly when chips begin to melt. Sprinkle remaining almonds evenly over top of chocolate and gently press into chocolate layer.

4. Let harden about 1 hour. Cut or break into pieces. Enjoy!

OREO CHOCOLATE TRUFFLES

You just can't go wrong with Oreo cookies. They're a vegan junk food staple. Here I turn them into creamy truffles. Easy to make—and even easier to devour!

» MAKES 2 DOZEN TRUFFLES «

2 cups finely crushed Oreo cookies

1 (8-ounce) container vegan cream cheese, softened

1 (12-ounce) package vegan chocolate chips

1 teaspoon coconut oil

1. In a large bowl, combine cookie crumbs and cream cheese until very well combined. Refrigerate at least 1 hour.

2. In a medium saucepan over medium-high heat, melt chocolate and coconut oil, stirring constantly until smooth. Remove from heat.

3. Shape crumb mixture into 1" balls.

4. Dip refrigerated balls into chocolate coating completely and place on parchment paper. Refrigerate until firm.

COCONUT ALMOND CHOCOLATE CANDY BARS

1 cup sugar

¾ cup water

¼ teaspoon salt

1 (8-ounce) package unsweetened coconut

½ teaspoon vanilla extract

¼ teaspoon almond extract

½ cup whole almonds

⅔ cup vegan chocolate chips

If you love Almond Joy candy bars (which aren't vegan), give these babies a whirl. You will not be disappointed.

1. Lightly grease a cookie sheet.

2. In a large saucepan over high heat, bring sugar and water to a boil; cook until sugar is completely dissolved. Add salt and coconut to the pan. Lower heat to medium-high and continue to cook until the water has evaporated, about 10–15 minutes. Remove from heat. Stir in vanilla and almond extracts.

3. Press coconut mixture onto prepared sheet and press into a large square. While still warm, press an almond into the coconut about every 2".

4. In a small microwave-safe bowl, microwave chocolate chips 15 seconds at a time, stirring after each interval until melted and smooth. Pour evenly over coconut and almonds. Cool on the counter. Cut into bars.

LAYERED CRACKERS CANDY BARS

» MAKES 1 DOZEN
BARS «

30 saltine crackers

½ cup graham cracker crumbs

1 cup packed brown sugar

½ cup vegan butter

¼ cup nondairy milk

1 teaspoon vanilla extract

⅔ cup vegan chocolate chips

2 tablespoons peanut butter

Perfect for when a snack attack hits, the convenience store is closed, and all you have on hand is a box of saltines. In roughly an hour, you can have delicious candy bars!

1. Line an 8" × 8" baking dish with parchment paper.

2. Arrange half the saltine crackers in prepared baking dish.

3. In a large saucepan, combine graham cracker crumbs, brown sugar, butter, and milk. Bring to a boil over medium-high heat and allow to boil 5 minutes, stirring constantly. Remove from heat and stir in vanilla.

4. Pour mixture over saltines in dish. Top with remaining saltines.

5. In a small microwave-safe bowl, microwave chocolate chips and peanut butter in 15-second intervals, stirring between each interval until mixture is melted and smooth. Pour evenly over crackers. Refrigerate until set, about 1 hour. Cut into bars.

ULTIMATE PEANUT BUTTER CHOCOLATE CHIP COOKIES

This soft variety of cookie melts in your mouth. Crunchy peanut butter gives the cookies some texture, and the chocolate chips take them to the ultimately delicious category. Best warm from the oven, but they stay pliable for a few days stored airtight.

1 cup crunchy peanut butter

¾ cup packed light brown sugar

¾ cup sugar

1 cup vegan butter

2 tablespoons water mixed with 2 tablespoons ground flaxseeds

1 teaspoon vanilla extract

1 teaspoon baking soda

½ teaspoon baking powder

1 teaspoon salt

2½ cups flour

1½ cups vegan chocolate chips

1. Preheat oven to 350°F.

2. In a mixer, combine peanut butter, sugars, and butter. Mix on high speed until light and fluffy. Add water-flax mixture and vanilla; mix to incorporate.

3. In a separate medium bowl, sift together baking soda, baking powder, salt, and flour.

4. Stir flour mixture into butter mixture with a wooden spoon just until a uniform dough forms. Fold in chocolate chips.

5. Drop by heaping teaspoonful onto an ungreased baking sheet. Bake 8–12 minutes until just golden. Cool on a rack.

LIME CHEESECAKE TRUFFLES

» MAKES 2 DOZEN
TRUFFLES «

1 (8-ounce) container vegan
    cream cheese

3¼ cups powdered sugar

Zest of 2 medium limes

3 tablespoons fresh lime juice

1 (12-ounce) package vegan
    white chocolate chips

1 teaspoon virgin coconut oil

½ cup graham cracker crumbs

1 tablespoon sugar

For when you're feeling a bit more refined, I present this truly unique white-chocolate truffle with a tart zing of lime and a sweet graham cracker coating.

«------------------------------»

1. In a mixer, combine cream cheese, powdered sugar, lime zest, and lime juice; mix until completely combined. Refrigerate mixture until truffle mix is firm enough to form into balls, about 30 minutes.

2. Line a baking sheet with parchment paper. Using a melon baller or your hands, form truffle mix into 1" balls and place on prepared sheet. Refrigerate 1 hour.

3. In a heavy-bottomed medium saucepan over medium heat, melt white chocolate with the coconut oil, stirring until completely melted.

4. Place graham cracker crumbs and sugar in a shallow dish and mix together. Using two forks, dip each truffle into the melted chocolate, turning to coat completely, and then dip half of each coated truffle in the crumbs; set on parchment sheet to set.

5. Keep truffles in the refrigerator.

PEANUT BUTTER TRUFFLES

Another vegan variation on the classic flavors of Reese's peanut butter cups, this time in truffle form for quick and simple inhalation! (These don't last very long in my house.)

1. Line a baking sheet with waxed paper.

2. In a medium bowl, combine peanut butter, butter, and powdered sugar, stirring until very smooth.

3. Roll into 1" balls. Place on prepared baking sheet.

4. Melt chocolate and shortening in a medium heavy saucepan over medium-low heat, stirring constantly. Using two forks, dip balls into chocolate, turning to cover on all sides. Roll in nuts and set truffles on prepared baking sheet to allow chocolate to set.

5. Refrigerate leftovers.

1 cup chunky peanut butter

2 tablespoons vegan butter

1 cup powdered sugar

1 (12-ounce) package vegan chocolate chips

1 tablespoon nonhydrogenated vegetable shortening

1½ cups chopped nuts (almonds or pecans)

PEANUT BUTTER FUDGE

1 teaspoon vanilla extract

¾ cup peanut butter

1 cup sugar

1 cup packed brown sugar

½ cup soy creamer

2 tablespoons light corn syrup

½ teaspoon salt

Peanut butter in all its delightful forms! Here you have old-fashioned flavor and creamy, fudgy texture. Make sure to cool completely before cutting or you'll end up with a ball of fudge instead of squares.

1. Lightly grease a 9" × 9" baking dish.

2. In a small bowl, mix together vanilla and peanut butter.

3. In a large saucepan over medium-high heat, bring sugar, brown sugar, soy creamer, corn syrup, and salt to a boil, stirring constantly. Once at a full boil, cover and cook 1 minute.

4. Remove cover; do not stir. Continue cooking until a candy thermometer reaches 240°F. (You can also test for this temperature by dropping a pea-sized amount of fudge into a glass of ice water; the fudge should easily form into a ball in the water and melt as you remove it from the water.) Without stirring, spoon on peanut butter mixed with vanilla. Remove pan from heat and allow to cool on the counter 20 minutes.

5. After 20 minutes, stir fudge with a wooden spoon until it begins to thicken and become creamy, about 2–3 minutes.

6. Spoon into prepared baking dish and smooth the top. Cool completely before cutting into squares.

VANILLA FUDGE

Did you know there are at least nine varieties of vanilla, each with distinct flavors, from places as far-flung as Papua New Guinea? If you really love the taste of vanilla, you may want to seek out something more exotic to try in this recipe, which yields a creamy fudge with a walnut crunch.

2½ cups sugar

¾ cup Vegan Sour Cream (see Chapter 6)

½ cup light corn syrup

3 tablespoons vegan butter

1½ teaspoons vanilla extract

¾ cup chopped walnuts

« – »

1. Lightly grease a 9" × 9" baking dish.

2. In a large saucepan over medium-high heat, bring sugar, sour cream, corn syrup, and butter to a boil, stirring constantly. Once at a full boil, cover and cook 1 minute.

3. Remove cover, do not stir. Continue cooking until a candy thermometer reaches 240°F. (You can also test for this temperature by dropping a pea-sized amount of fudge into a glass of ice water; the fudge should easily form into a ball in the water and flatten as you remove it from the water.) Remove pan from heat and allow to cool on the counter 20 minutes.

4. After 20 minutes, stir fudge with a wooden spoon until it begins to thicken and become creamy, about 2–3 minutes. Stir in vanilla and walnuts.

5. Spoon into prepared baking dish and smooth the top. Cool completely before cutting into squares.

S'MORES SQUARES

Who needs a campfire when you can make these from the comfort of your home? Familiar flavors in a familiar place set the stage for proper enjoyment of "junk."

½ cup vegan butter

1 teaspoon vanilla extract

1 cup graham cracker crumbs

¾ cup brown sugar

1 (2.5-ounce) package vegan mini marshmallows

1 cup vegan semisweet chocolate chips

1. Preheat oven to 350°F. Line a 9" × 9" baking dish with foil and lightly grease.

2. In a medium saucepan over medium-high heat, melt butter. Remove from heat and add vanilla.

3. In a large bowl, mix graham cracker crumbs, brown sugar, marshmallows, and chocolate chips. Pour butter over mixture and mix well. Pour into prepared baking dish.

4. Bake 15 minutes. Allow to cool completely. Use foil to remove bars from pan and cut into squares.

SCOTTISH SHORTBREAD DIPPED *in* CHOCOLATE

» MAKES 1 DOZEN COOKIES «

2 cups vegan butter

1 cup sugar

2 teaspoons vanilla extract

4 cups flour

1 (12-ounce) package vegan chocolate chips

1 tablespoon coconut oil

Vaguely reminiscent of the ubiquitous NYC black-and-white cookies, here you've got a buttery, crunchy short-bread baked in a wedge and dipped in chocolate. Six ingredients, and you're well on your way to noshing...

1. Preheat oven to 275°F. Have ready an ungreased baking sheet.

2. In a mixer or by hand, cream butter and sugar until light and fluffy. Add vanilla.

3. Add flour 1 cup at a time, mixing thoroughly after each addition.

4. On a floured surface, roll out cookie dough into a circle about ½" thick. Cut into wedges, place on cookie sheet, and prick with fork.

5. Bake 45 minutes or until very lightly browned.

6. Line a baking sheet with parchment paper.

7. In a medium saucepan over medium-low heat, melt chocolate chips and coconut oil, stirring constantly. Cool slightly until chocolate is just warm to the touch. Holding the point of each cookie, dip halfway into chocolate and allow excess chocolate to drip off. Place cookie on prepared baking sheet to set.

RED VELVET WHOOPIE PIES

Red velvet is all the rage these days, so why not take the popular cake and turn it into whoopie pies? Because, really, when it comes down to it, all junk food should be portable.

« - »

1. Preheat oven to 400°F. Line a cookie sheet with parchment paper.

2. In a small bowl, add apple cider vinegar and flaxseeds to soy milk, then set aside.

3. In a mixer, cream butter, sugar, and vanilla.

4. In a medium bowl, sift together flour, cocoa powder, baking soda, and salt, or use a whisk to combine the dry ingredients. Add dry ingredients to the mixer bowl. Add food coloring to soy milk mixture and then add to the mixer bowl. Mix until smooth.

5. Drop by the heaping tablespoonful onto prepared cookie sheet, slightly flattening.

6. Bake 8 minutes. Cool completely.

Filling

1. In a mixer, beat powdered sugar, shortening, butter, cornstarch, and vanilla until light and fluffy.

2. For each whoopie pie, spread a tablespoon of filling on one flattened side of a cookie and sandwich it with another cookie, flat sides together.

>> **MAKES 10 PIES** «

- 1 tablespoon apple cider vinegar
- 1 tablespoon ground flaxseeds
- 1 cup soy milk
- ⅔ cup vegan butter
- 1 cup sugar
- 1 teaspoon vanilla extract
- 2¼ cups flour
- ¼ cup cocoa powder
- 1 teaspoon baking soda
- 1 teaspoon salt
- 2 tablespoons vegan-derived red food coloring

- 2 cups powdered sugar
- ½ cup Spectrum nonhydrogenated vegetable shortening
- 2 tablespoons vegan butter
- 1 tablespoon cornstarch
- 1 teaspoon vanilla extract

CHOCOLATE MINT WHOOPIE PIES

1 tablespoon apple cider vinegar

1 tablespoon ground flaxseeds

1 cup soy milk

⅔ cup vegan butter

1 cup sugar

1 teaspoon vanilla extract

2¼ cups flour

¾ cup cocoa powder

1 teaspoon baking soda

1 teaspoon salt

2 cups powdered sugar

½ cup Spectrum nonhydrogenated vegetable shortening

2 tablespoons vegan butter

1 tablespoon cornstarch

2 teaspoons mint extract

Chocolate outside, minty inside—pair alongside some vegan mint chocolate-chip ice cream if you really want to get crazy.

1. Preheat oven to 400°F. Line a cookie sheet with parchment paper.

2. In a small bowl, add apple cider vinegar and flaxseeds to soy milk, then set aside.

3. In a mixer, cream butter, sugar, and vanilla.

4. In a medium bowl, sift together flour, cocoa powder, baking soda, and salt, or use a whisk to combine dry ingredients. Add dry ingredients to the mixer bowl and pour in milk mixture. Mix until smooth.

5. Drop by the heaping tablespoonful onto prepared cookie sheet, slightly flattening as you go.

6. Bake 8 minutes. Cool completely.

Filling

1. In a mixer, beat powdered sugar, shortening, butter, cornstarch, and mint extract until light and fluffy.

2. For each whoopie pie, spread a tablespoon of filling on one flattened side of cookie and sandwich it with another cookie, flat sides together.

GINGERBREAD SANDWICH COOKIES
with VANILLA CREAM

Terrifically flavorful spicy cookie with a creamy filling, this is like the adult version of an Oreo cookie. Not that there's anything wrong with Oreo cookies, but this will appeal to a more sophisticated palate. Don't omit the molasses; it's a key ingredient.

» MAKES 1 DOZEN COOKIES «

2 tablespoons ground flaxseeds

¼ cup water

2 cups flour

½ teaspoon baking soda

½ teaspoon baking powder

1½ teaspoons ground ginger

1 teaspoon ground cinnamon

½ teaspoon salt

¾ cup vegan butter

½ cup sugar

¼ cup molasses

1. Line two baking sheets with parchment paper.

2. In a small bowl, mix together flaxseeds and water, then set aside.

3. In a medium bowl, sift flour, baking soda, baking powder, ginger, cinnamon, and salt.

4. In a mixer, cream butter, sugar, and molasses until fluffy. Add flaxseed mixture and mix well. Add dry ingredients and mix well.

5. Divide dough in half, shape each half into a log, and tamp edges on counter to make flat edges on each cylinder. Wrap in plastic and refrigerate 1 hour.

6. Preheat oven to 350°F.

7. Unwrap log and cut with a sharp, thin knife into ¼" rounds. Place 2" apart on prepared baking sheet.

8. Bake 10–12 minutes. Slip cookies off the tray with parchment and cool.

Filling

½ cup vegan butter

2 cups powdered sugar

2 teaspoons vanilla extract

1. In a stand mixer or by hand with a whisk, cream butter until light and fluffy. Gradually add powdered sugar until it is all incorporated. Add vanilla and beat about 3 minutes.

2. Spoon about a tablespoon of filling between each pair of cookies.

POWDERED PECAN NUGGET COOKIES

» MAKES 1 DOZEN
COOKIES «

2 cups vegan butter

¼ cup sugar

2 teaspoons vanilla extract

2 cups flour

1 cup pecans, chopped

2 cups powdered sugar

Is it a ball? Is it a cookie? The debate rages on, although one thing's for sure: they belong in your belly!

«– –»

1. Preheat oven to 350°F.

2. In a mixer, cream butter and sugar until fluffy. Mix in vanilla.

3. Add flour and mix just to combine. Mix in pecans.

4. Form dough into walnut-sized balls and place 1" apart on an ungreased cookie sheet.

5. Bake 15 minutes or until barely golden brown.

6. While still hot from the oven, roll cookies in powdered sugar. Cool completely and roll in powdered sugar again.

COCONUT OATMEAL COOKIES

» MAKES 2 DOZEN
COOKIES «

½ cup vegan butter

1 cup brown sugar

1 teaspoon vanilla extract

¼ cup applesauce

½ teaspoon salt

1 cup flour

1 teaspoon baking powder

1 teaspoon baking soda

1¼ cups old-fashioned oats

1½ cups shredded coconut, unsweetened

Some people are in the crisp camp when it comes to oatmeal cookies; others are in the chewy camp. Those in the latter group will adore these cookies, which are traditional but for the addition of coconut.

«– –»

1. Preheat oven to 375°F. Lightly grease a cookie sheet.

2. In a large bowl, cream the butter, brown sugar, and vanilla until fluffy. Add in applesauce and mix to combine.

3. In a medium bowl, sift together salt, flour, baking powder, and baking soda. Add to the butter mixture and mix well to combine. Stir in oats and coconut.

4. Shape into 1½" balls and place on prepared cookie sheet 2" apart. Slightly flatten with the bottom of a glass dipped in sugar to prevent sticking.

5. Bake 10 minutes or until just golden brown.

NO-BAKE ORANGE COOKIES

These taste like a baked cookie, citrusy and crispy, but you can give your oven a break.

« – »

1. In a large bowl, mix all ingredients until well blended.
2. Shape into 1" balls.
3. Store in an airtight container and use within 5 days.

1 cup powdered sugar

⅓ cup frozen orange juice concentrate

¼ cup corn syrup

¼ cup vegan butter

4 cups graham cracker crumbs

1 cup chopped almonds

CHOCOLATE CHIP MACADAMIA NUT COOKIES

Get your ice-cold glass of soy milk ready for dunking when these come out of the oven piping hot and melty. So good!

« – »

1. Preheat oven to 350°F. Place a sheet of parchment paper on a cookie sheet.
2. In a small bowl, combine flaxseeds and water; set aside.
3. In a mixer, cream butter, sugar, and brown sugar until fluffy. Add vanilla. Mix in flaxseed-water mixture to combine.
4. In a medium bowl, sift together flour, baking soda, and salt. Add flour mixture to the mixer bowl and mix until completely combined. Stir in chocolate chips and macadamia nuts.
5. Drop cookies by the heaping tablespoonfuls onto an ungreased cookie sheet.
6. Bake 8–10 minutes.

2 tablespoons ground flaxseeds

¼ cup water

1 cup plus 2 tablespoons vegan butter

1 cup sugar

1 cup packed brown sugar

1 teaspoon vanilla extract

2½ cups flour

1½ teaspoons baking soda

1 teaspoon salt

1 (12-ounce) package vegan semisweet chocolate chips

1 cup macadamia nut halves

SUGAR COOKIES

¼ cup nondairy milk

2 tablespoons ground flaxseeds

2 cups sugar

¾ cup vegan butter

1 teaspoon vanilla extract

3 cups plus 2 tablespoons flour

2 teaspoons baking powder

½ teaspoon salt

½ cup sugar

Pick your pleasure: you can either make these with cookie-cutter shapes for a crisper cookie or simply form the dough into logs before refrigerating and slice it for a chewier cookie.

« – »

1. In a small bowl, mix milk and flaxseeds; set aside.

2. In a mixer, beat sugar and butter until fluffy. Add the vanilla and flaxseed mixture and mix well.

3. In a medium bowl, sift flour, baking powder, and salt; add to mixer bowl and mix until well combined.

4. Divide the dough into thirds and flatten each into a disk. Wrap in plastic and refrigerate at least 1 hour.

5. Preheat oven to 400°F. Lightly grease a cookie sheet or line with parchment paper.

6. Use one disk at a time, keeping the other disks refrigerated. Roll out dough on a floured surface or between sheets of plastic to ⅛" thickness. Use cookie cutters or a biscuit cutter to shape cookies. Place 2" apart on prepared cookie sheet.

7. Sprinkle with sugar before baking or leave plain for decorating with icing.

POTATO CHIP COOKIES

If you thought potato chips were merely meant to be chomped on straight from the bag or dunked in dip, think again. We're getting creative, folks! Here, I fold them, along with peanuts, into a cookie.

1 cup brown sugar

1 cup white sugar

1 cup nonhydrogenated vegetable shortening

4 tablespoons vegan butter, softened

1 teaspoon vanilla extract

2¼ cups flour

1 teaspoon baking soda

3 cups potato chips, crushed

½ cup peanuts, chopped

1 tablespoon sugar

1. Preheat oven to 350°F. Line a cookie sheet with parchment paper.

2. In a stand mixer or by hand, beat brown sugar, white sugar, shortening, and butter until fluffy, about 5 minutes. Mix in vanilla.

3. In a small bowl, sift flour and baking soda. Add to butter mixture and mix until well combined. Stir in 2 cups crushed potato chips and peanuts.

4. In a small bowl, stir together remaining crushed chips and 1 tablespoon sugar.

5. Using a heaping tablespoonful of dough, roll each cookie into a ball and press the bottom only into the potato chip–sugar mixture. Place on prepared baking sheet, chip-covered side down.

6. Bake 10–12 minutes or until just light golden brown.

CINNAMON ROLL COOKIES

1 recipe Sugar Cookies dough
(see recipe in this chapter),
divided into 2 disks and
refrigerated 1 hour

½ cup vegan butter

½ cup Sucanat or organic
brown sugar

2 teaspoons ground cinnamon

With these luscious little treats, it's all about the icing.
Enjoy for breakfast (or anytime, really)!

« – »

1. Use one disk of cookie dough at a time, leaving the other
refrigerated. Roll dough into an approximately 12" × 5" rectangle on a floured surface or between layers of plastic wrap.

2. In a small bowl, combine butter, Sucanat or brown sugar,
and cinnamon. Spread half of this mixture onto cookie dough
rectangle. Roll, using long end of dough, into a log keeping it
tight and even. Wrap in plastic; repeat with the rest of cookie
dough and filling mixture. Refrigerate logs at least 1 hour.

3. Preheat oven to 350°F. Line a baking sheet with lightly
greased parchment paper.

4. Using a thin sharp knife, cut dough into ½" slices and place
on prepared cookie sheet.

5. Bake 10 minutes or until light golden brown. Allow to cool
2 minutes on the cookie sheet, then transfer to a wire rack to
cool completely. Top with Icing.

Icing

1 (8-ounce) container vegan
cream cheese

¾ cup powdered sugar

4 tablespoons nondairy milk

1. Beat cream cheese and powdered sugar together, adding
milk 1 tablespoon at a time until frosting is thick but pourable.

2. Drizzle over cooled cookies.

RUGELACH

Here it is. The classic deli cookie, demystified. Feel free to sub out the apricot jam with any kind of jam that you're craving.

« - »

1. In a large bowl, mix butter, cream cheese, and flour. Divide into four balls, wrap with plastic, and refrigerate 2 hours.

2. Preheat oven to 375°F. Line a cookie sheet with parchment paper.

3. On a floured surface, roll each ball into a 10"-diameter circle. With a knife, cut each circle into 10–12 wedges. On each wedge, spread jam evenly in a thin layer.

4. In a small bowl, mix sugar, walnuts, and cinnamon. Sprinkle about a teaspoon over jam on each wedge.

5. Roll gently from the wide part of wedge to the point. Place on prepared baking sheet. Sprinkle with any remaining cinnamon-sugar mixture.

6. Bake 35 minutes or until golden brown.

» **MAKES 2 DOZEN COOKIES** «

1 cup vegan butter

1 (8-ounce) container vegan cream cheese

1 cup flour

½ cup apricot jam

⅓ cup sugar

½ cup finely chopped walnuts

1 tablespoon ground cinnamon

BUTTERFINGER CHUNK COOKIES

In this recipe, you make your own Butterfinger chunks, then bake them into a totally decadent cookie. A quick web search should turn up vendors who carry Chick-O-Stick candy, but expect to have it shipped, as it's not available everywhere.

» MAKES 1 DOZEN COOKIES «

1 cup vegan chocolate chips

1 tablespoon coconut oil

2 cups Chick-O-Stick candy, broken into marble-sized chunks

1 tablespoon ground flaxseeds

¼ cup water

1 cup vegan butter

½ cup sugar

½ cup packed brown sugar

1 teaspoon vanilla extract

2 cups all-purpose flour

1 teaspoon baking soda

« - »

1. Line a baking sheet with parchment paper.

2. In a small saucepan over medium-high heat, melt chocolate and coconut oil, stirring constantly until smooth. Remove from heat. Stir in Chick-O-Stick candy and mix to coat all pieces. Pour out onto prepared baking sheet. Refrigerate until chocolate is set. Break up into small pieces.

3. Preheat oven to 350°F. Line another baking sheet with parchment paper.

4. In a small bowl, mix flaxseeds and water; set aside.

5. In a stand mixer or by hand, cream butter, sugar, brown sugar, and vanilla until light and fluffy. Stir in flaxseed mixture. Mix in flour and baking soda until dough forms. Stir in candy pieces.

6. Form cookies into 2" balls and place 2" apart on prepared cookie sheet.

7. Bake 10–12 minutes or until edges are light golden brown. Let cool on cookie sheet 2 minutes, then transfer to a wire rack to completely cool.

MINI CHOCOLATE BABKA

¼ cup 100°F water

½ ounce (2 envelopes) dry yeast

¼ cup plus 1 teaspoon sugar, divided

2½ cups flour

1 teaspoon salt

4 tablespoons vegan butter, room temperature

¼ cup vegetable oil

2 tablespoons ground flaxseed mixed with 4 tablespoons water

⅓ cup chocolate chips

FILLING

½ cup vegan butter, room temperature

¼ cup unsweetened cocoa

¾ cup sugar

½ cup chopped walnuts

Babka is a yeast bread with an inner swirl of cinnamon, chocolate, or fruit and nuts. In this mini chocolate version, the dough is rolled cinnamon-roll style and cut into disks that are baked in cupcake tins.

1. Place 100°F water, yeast, and 1 teaspoon sugar into a large mixing bowl or the bowl of a stand mixer; let proof 10 minutes.

2. Add ¼ cup sugar, flour, salt, butter, oil, and flaxseed mixture. Combine with the dough hook attachment of a stand mixer or by hand until all the ingredients are mixed and dough is smooth. Cover bowl with a towel and let rise 1½ hours.

3. Preheat oven to 325°F. Grease two (12-cup) muffin trays.

4. Make the filling: in a medium bowl, mix butter, cocoa, sugar, and walnuts, mix until combined. Set aside.

5. Divide dough in half. Sprinkle surface with a little flour. With a rolling pin, roll each piece of dough into a 9" × 12" rectangle. Spread half the chocolate filling all the way to the edges. Sprinkle half the chocolate chips all over the chocolate filling and roll up tightly the long way. Repeat with the other half of dough.

6. Cut into ½" slices and place one into each of the muffin cups, cut side up. You will have about 24 slices. Repeat with the rest of the dough.

7. Bake 20 minutes or until golden brown.

CHAPTER 10

Grab 'n' Go Sweets

• Sinful Bars, Brownies, and More •

BLUEBERRY CRUMBLE BARS

Don't let the ample amount of fresh berries in this dish fool you; with more than 1 cup of sugar and 1 cup of butter, it's still full-on junk food.

« – »

» MAKES 8–10 BARS «

1 tablespoon ground flaxseeds
¼ cup water
3¼ cups flour
1½ cups sugar, divided
1 teaspoon baking powder
1 cup vegan butter
4 cups fresh blueberries or blackberries
1 teaspoon lemon zest
1 tablespoon cornstarch

1. Preheat oven to 350°F. Line a 9" × 13" baking pan with foil, lightly greased.

2. In a small bowl, combine flaxseeds and water; set aside 5 minutes.

3. In a mixer or by hand, combine flour, 1 cup sugar, baking powder, butter, and flaxseed mixture until evenly combined and crumbly.

4. Press half the crumble mixture into prepared pan.

5. In a medium bowl, mix together the berries, lemon zest, ½ cup sugar, and cornstarch. Spoon on top of crust. Top with the remainder of crumble mixture.

6. Bake 40–45 minutes or until crumble is lightly browned.

7. Cool completely. Use foil to lift crumble out of pan and cut into bars.

HAWAIIAN PINEAPPLE COCONUT BARS

1 (20-ounce) can pineapple
   chunks, drained and chopped

4 tablespoons cornstarch

½ cup sugar

½ cup vegan butter, melted

2 cups brown sugar

2 cups flaked coconut

2 cups flour

1 teaspoon salt

When you enjoy these bars while wearing a lei, it increases the flavor exponentially! You know, really get in the spirit.

1. Preheat oven to 350°F. Line a 9" × 13" baking dish with parchment paper.

2. In a medium saucepan, combine pineapple, cornstarch, and sugar. Cook, stirring constantly, until mixture becomes thick; remove from heat.

3. In a medium bowl, mix butter and brown sugar. Add coconut, flour, and salt; mix until well combined.

4. Press half of coconut mixture into prepared baking dish. Bake 10 minutes.

5. Spread pineapple evenly over crust. Crumble the remainder of coconut mixture over pineapple and press lightly.

6. Bake 30 minutes or until top is golden brown. Cool completely before cutting into bars.

ALMOND JOY BAR CAKE

Dense like a brownie, this cake is great for when you feel like a nut. Candy bar craving, solved.

2 tablespoons ground flaxseeds

¼ cup water

¾ cup vegan butter

1 teaspoon almond extract

2 cups sugar

1¼ cups flour

½ cup cocoa powder

1 teaspoon baking powder

1 teaspoon salt

1½ cups flaked coconut

1 cup chopped almonds

1. Preheat oven to 350°F. Lightly grease a 9" × 13" baking dish.

2. In a small bowl, mix flaxseeds and water; set aside.

3. In a mixer, cream butter, almond extract, and sugar until light and fluffy. Add flaxseed mixture and mix.

4. In a medium bowl, sift together flour, cocoa powder, baking powder, and salt. Add to the creamed butter mixture.

5. Pour half of batter into prepared baking dish and top with coconut and ¾ cup chopped almonds. Pour in the other half of batter. Sprinkle with remaining almonds.

6. Bake 30 minutes. Cool completely before cutting.

PEANUT BUTTER CUP COOKIE BARS

» MAKES 8–10 BARS «

1½ cups finely crushed peanut butter sandwich cookies (such as Nutter Butter cookies)

¼ cup plus 2 tablespoons vegan butter, melted, divided

½ cup coconut oil, melted, divided

1½ cups peanut butter, divided

1½ cups powdered sugar

1 (12-ounce) package vegan semisweet chocolate chips

Yet another pairing of two of the most revered flavors in the junk food universe: chocolate and peanut butter. In this case, you get a peanut butter cookie crust, followed by a thick peanut butter layer topped with chocolate. A total Reese's rip-off!

1. Line a 9" × 9" baking dish with parchment paper or waxed paper.

2. Make the crust: in a medium bowl, combine the crushed cookies, ¼ cup butter, and ¼ cup coconut oil. Press into prepared dish.

3. Make the filling: in the same bowl, combine 1 cup peanut butter, powdered sugar, ¼ cup coconut oil, and 2 tablespoons butter, stirring until smooth. Spoon onto crust, patting evenly to distribute. Refrigerate 30 minutes.

4. In a small saucepan over medium-low heat, melt the chocolate chips with remaining ½ cup peanut butter, stirring constantly.

5. Pour over filling layer and refrigerate until set enough to cut into bars, about 4 hours.

PECAN PIE BARS

A portable version of the perennial holiday favorite. If you're feeling extra junky, melt some vegan chocolate chips to drizzle over the top of this before it is set out to cool. Yum!

« – »

1. Preheat oven to 350°F. Lightly grease a 9" × 9" baking dish.

2. In a medium bowl using a whisk or a fork, combine flour, 2 tablespoons brown sugar, and ½ cup butter until a dough forms. Press into prepared baking dish.

3. Bake 15 minutes.

4. In a medium bowl, mix ½ cup brown sugar, applesauce, corn syrup, pecans, ½ cup melted butter, vanilla, and salt. Pour this mixture over crust.

5. Bake 25 minutes or until edges are light golden brown. Cool completely before cutting into bars.

» MAKES 8–10 BARS «

- 1⅓ cups flour
- ½ cup plus 2 tablespoons brown sugar, divided
- 1 cup vegan butter, melted and divided
- ¼ cup applesauce
- ½ cup light corn syrup
- ½ cup pecans, finely chopped
- 1 teaspoon vanilla extract
- ½ teaspoon salt

NO-BAKE CHOCOLATE CHUNK BANANA PEANUT BALLS

Got four ingredients? How about four minutes? Then you could have a terrific snack with virtually no effort.

« – »

1. Mix graham cracker crumbs, banana, peanut butter, and chocolate chips until thoroughly combined.

2. Shape into 1½" balls.

» MAKES 12 BALLS «

- 2 cups graham cracker crumbs
- 1 medium banana, mashed
- ½ cup chunky peanut butter
- ½ cup vegan chocolate chips

GLAZED LEMON BREAD

½ cup vegan butter

½ cup applesauce

1 cup sugar

Zest of 3 medium lemons (zest lemons before juicing)

5 tablespoons lemon juice, divided

1½ cups flour

1 teaspoon baking powder

1 teaspoon salt

½ cup powdered sugar

Enjoy for breakfast, lunch, dinner, snack time, or anytime. The tart flavor is offset by the sweet glaze that melts into the bread when it's right out of the oven—delicious!

1. Preheat oven to 350°F. Grease and lightly flour a 9" × 5" loaf pan.

2. In a stand mixer or by hand, beat butter, applesauce, sugar, lemon zest, and 3 tablespoons lemon juice until very well mixed.

3. In a medium bowl, sift together flour, baking powder, and salt. Add to butter mixture and stir just until combined; do not overmix.

4. Pour into prepared loaf pan.

5. Bake 45–50 minutes or until a knife comes out clean.

6. In a small bowl, mix remaining 2 tablespoons lemon juice with powdered sugar. When lemon bread is hot from the oven, drizzle with lemon glaze. Cool completely before cutting.

PB&J BARS

Be careful if you have kids, because once you make these cookies—a sugar cookie with strawberry filling and a peanut butter crumble—they'll never go back to eating regular PB&J sandwiches again. (Consider yourself warned.)

<< – >>

1. Preheat oven to 375°F. Line a 9" × 9" baking dish with foil and lightly grease.

2. Press two-thirds of the Sugar Cookies dough into prepared pan. Spread with jam, leaving a ¼" border along the edges free of jam.

3. In a medium bowl, mix the peanut butter and powdered sugar until completely combined. Add the remainder of the cookie dough and granola cereal. Crumble this mixture over jam layer.

4. Bake 25–30 minutes or until topping turns golden brown. Cool completely. Use foil to lift from pan and cut into bars.

>> **MAKES 10–12 BARS** <<

1 recipe Sugar Cookies dough (see Chapter 9)

⅔ cup strawberry jam

¾ cup peanut butter

¼ cup powdered sugar

½ cup granola cereal

REAL-DEAL BAKLAVA

3⅓ cups chopped nuts (almonds, walnuts, or pistachios, or a combination of each)

1 cup sugar

1 teaspoon ground cinnamon

1 pound frozen phyllo dough (check for vegan ingredients or look for The Fillo Factory brand), defrosted and covered with a damp towel

1 cup vegan butter, melted

Phyllo dough, which is the essence of this traditional dessert with cinnamon and nutty syrup-soaked layers, can be easily made from scratch, but you can save time by buying the dough prepared. Just be sure to check the ingredients to make sure they're not sneaking in any animal products.

« – »

1. Preheat oven to 350°F. Lightly grease a 9" × 13" baking dish.

2. In a medium bowl, mix the nuts, sugar, and cinnamon.

3. Using kitchen shears, cut the entire stack of phyllo dough in half so that the sheets fit in the baking dish.

4. Lay one sheet of phyllo in the baking dish and brush with melted butter; keep the stack of waiting dough covered as you work. Repeat 6 times. Spoon about 3 tablespoons of the nut mixture in an even layer. Top the nut mixture with two sheets of phyllo, then another 3 tablespoons of nut mixture. Repeat with two layers of butter-brushed dough and nut mixture until you run out of nuts. The last layers will be about five or six layers of butter-brushed phyllo.

5. Using a very sharp knife, cut through the layers of dough, making a pattern of several diamonds almost but not quite down to the bottom of dough layers.

6. Bake 50 minutes. Remove from oven.

Sugar Syrup

1 cup water

1 cup sugar

½ cup agave

2 tablespoons lemon juice

1. While the baklava is baking, place water, sugar, agave, and lemon juice in a medium saucepan; bring to a boil, stirring to dissolve the sugar. Once syrup reaches a boil, turn the heat down to medium-low and simmer about 20 minutes. Allow syrup to cool completely before the next step.

2. When the baklava comes out of the oven, evenly pour Sugar Syrup over the baklava. Allow to cool completely.

HAZELNUT CHOCOLATE BAKLAVA

This tastes like a marriage of baklava and Nutella. The latter isn't vegan, so this should satisfy your chocolate-hazelnut craving, lickety-split.

« - »

1. Preheat oven to 350°F. Lightly grease a 9" × 13" baking dish.

2. Make the sugar syrup: place water, sugar, agave, and lemon juice in a medium saucepan; bring to a boil, stirring to dissolve the sugar. Once syrup reaches a boil, turn the heat down to medium-low and simmer about 20 minutes. Allow syrup to cool completely before the next step.

3. In a medium bowl, mix the nuts, brown sugar, and chocolate chips.

4. Using kitchen shears, cut the entire stack of phyllo dough in half so that the sheets fit in the baking dish.

5. Lay one sheet of phyllo in the baking dish and brush with melted butter; keep the stack of waiting dough covered as you work. Repeat 6 times. Spoon about 3 tablespoons of the nut mixture in an even layer. Top the nut mixture with two sheets of phyllo, then another 3 tablespoons of nut mixture. Repeat with two layers of butter-brushed dough and nut mixture until you run out of nuts. The last layers will be about five or six layers of butter-brushed phyllo.

6. Using a very sharp knife, cut through the layers of dough, making a pattern of several diamonds almost but not quite down to the bottom of dough layers.

7. Bake 50 minutes. Remove from oven.

8. When the baklava comes out of the oven, evenly pour the prepared sugar syrup over the baklava. Allow to cool completely.

» **MAKES 2 DOZEN BARS** «

- 1 cup water
- 1 cup sugar
- ½ cup agave
- 1 tablespoon lemon juice
- 3⅓ cups chopped hazelnuts
- 1 cup packed brown sugar
- 1 cup vegan semisweet chocolate chips
- 1 pound frozen phyllo dough (check for vegan ingredients or try The Fillo Factory brand), defrosted and covered with a damp towel
- 1 cup vegan butter, melted

S'MORES CHOCOLATE CHIP COOKIE BARS

2 tablespoons ground
flaxseeds

¼ cup water

1 cup plus 2 tablespoons vegan
butter

1 cup sugar

1 cup packed brown sugar

1 teaspoon vanilla extract

2½ cups flour

1½ teaspoons baking soda

1 teaspoon salt

½ cup graham crackers,
broken into 1" pieces

½ cup vegan semisweet
chocolate chips

1 (2-ounce) package vegan
mini marshmallows

Like a blondie with a s'mores topping, bars like these bake up fast and are best enjoyed while the marshmallows are still totally melty.

« – »

1. Preheat oven to 350°F. Lightly grease a 9" × 9" baking dish.

2. In a small bowl, combine ground flaxseeds and water; set aside.

3. In a mixer, cream the butter, sugar, and brown sugar until fluffy. Add vanilla. Mix in flaxseed mixture.

4. In a medium bowl, sift together flour, baking soda, and salt. Add the flour mixture to the butter mixture and stir until completely combined.

5. Spoon dough into prepared baking dish and smooth top. Sprinkle with graham cracker pieces, chocolate chips, and marshmallows. Press into dough lightly.

6. Bake 30 minutes or until edges are golden brown and center is set.

PUMPKIN SHORTBREAD BARS

Make sure to let these set before cutting; that is, if you want to keep them neat. If you plan on eating straight from the pan, more power to you.

» MAKES 12–14 BARS «

1 recipe Scottish Shortbread dough, prepared but not baked (see Chapter 9)

1 (16-ounce) can pure pumpkin purée

⅔ cup nondairy milk

¾ cup packed brown sugar, divided

4 tablespoons cornstarch

1 tablespoon pumpkin pie spice

½ cup old-fashioned oats

¼ cup flour

¼ cup chopped pecans

½ teaspoon baking soda

¼ cup vegan butter, melted

1. Preheat oven to 350°F. Press Scottish Shortbread dough into a 9" × 13" baking dish. Bake 12 minutes.

2. In a mixer or by hand, beat pumpkin, milk, ½ cup brown sugar, cornstarch, and pumpkin pie spice until well combined. Pour over crust.

3. In a large bowl, combine oats, flour, ¼ cup brown sugar, pecans, baking soda, and butter. Crumble on top of filling.

4. Bake 25–30 minutes or until top is golden brown.

5. Cool completely before cutting. For best results, refrigerate overnight before cutting.

MAPLE PECAN SHORTBREAD BARS

Feel like you're traveling to Vermont or Canada as you enjoy these maple goodies.

» MAKES 12–14 BARS «

1 recipe Scottish Shortbread dough, unbaked (see Chapter 9)

2 cups coconut flakes

1 cup chopped pecans

1 cup pure maple syrup

1 teaspoon salt

1. Preheat oven to 350°F. Line a 9" × 13" baking dish with parchment paper.

2. Press Scottish Shortbread dough into prepared pan.

3. Bake 20–25 minutes or until lightly brown at edges.

4. In a medium saucepan over medium-high heat, mix coconut, pecans, syrup, and salt. Cook, stirring constantly, until liquid is absorbed by the coconut, about 5 minutes.

5. Spoon over crust, spreading evenly.

6. Bake about 10 minutes or until coconut becomes golden. Cut while still warm. Cool completely before removing from pan.

WHITE CHOCOLATE RASPBERRY BARS

This bakes in two stages but is deceivingly simple to make. Surprise a loved one who has a special sweet tooth for white chocolate with these rich, crunchy-fruity bars.

1 cup sugar

1 cup vegan butter

1 teaspoon vanilla extract

1 teaspoon salt

2½ cups flour

1 (12-ounce) package vegan white chocolate chips

½ cup applesauce

1 cup raspberry jam

1. Heat oven to 350°F. Grease a 9" × 9" baking dish.

2. In a mixer, combine sugar, butter, vanilla, and salt until completely combined. Add flour and mix until mixture resembles coarse crumbs. Set aside 1 cup of crumb mixture.

3. Heat half of white chocolate chips in a small saucepan over low heat just until melted.

4. Add applesauce and melted white chocolate to the remaining crumb mixture and mix until a dough forms. Press into prepared baking dish.

5. Bake 12 minutes.

6. Pour raspberry jam over crust and spread to within a ¼" of the edge. Sprinkle remaining white chocolate chips over jam. Top with reserved cup of crumbs.

7. Bake 25 minutes. Cool completely before cutting.

COCONUT CHERRY VODKA BARS

» MAKES 12–14
  BARS «

- 1½ cups coconut flakes
- ½ cup dried cherries
- ½ cup vanilla vodka
- 1¼ cups flour, divided
- ½ cup vegan butter
- ¼ cup sugar
- 2 tablespoons ground flaxseeds
- ⅔ cup sugar
- 1 teaspoon vanilla extract
- ½ cup water
- 1 teaspoon baking powder
- ½ teaspoon salt
- ¼ cup chopped almonds

If you don't have vanilla vodka on hand, you can always steep a vanilla bean in the vodka to infuse the flavor. Do this at least 2 hours before you plan to bake, longer if you're able. The result is a coconut-cherry-vanilla-vodka filling baked into a buttery-crisp bar.

« – »

1. In a small bowl, combine coconut, dried cherries, and vanilla vodka; steep 1 hour.

2. Preheat oven to 350°F. Line a 9" × 9" baking dish with parchment paper.

3. In a medium bowl, combine 1 cup flour, butter, and sugar until well blended. Press into bottom of prepared baking dish.

4. Bake 20 minutes.

5. In a medium bowl, mix ground flaxseeds, sugar, vanilla, and water, and stir well. Add ¼ cup flour, baking powder, and salt, mixing until well combined.

6. Drain vodka from cherries and coconut; shake in a colander to remove moisture.

7. Stir coconut, cherries, and nuts into flaxseed mixture. Pour over baked crust.

8. Bake 30–35 minutes or until golden brown.

CHOCOLATE-CHOCOLATE CHIP BANANA BREAD

A banana bread for chocolate lovers—a real junk-foodie take on the classic.

» MAKES 10–12 SERVINGS «

- -

1. Preheat oven to 350°F. Lightly grease a 9" × 5" loaf pan.

2. In a large bowl, mix together sugar, oil, flaxseeds, applesauce, banana, and vanilla.

3. In a medium bowl, sift together flour, cocoa powder, baking soda, and salt. Add to the banana mixture and stir until just combined; do not overmix. Fold in chopped chocolate.

4. Pour into prepared loaf pan.

5. Bake 50–60 minutes. Cool 10 minutes, then transfer to a wire rack. Cool completely before slicing.

1¼ cups sugar

½ cup oil

1 tablespoon ground flaxseeds

¼ cup applesauce

2 cups mashed banana

1 teaspoon vanilla extract

2 cups flour

¾ cup cocoa powder

1½ teaspoons baking soda

½ teaspoon salt

1 (3-ounce) vegan chocolate bar, roughly chopped

NO-BAKE BLUEBERRY CHEESECAKE BARS

2 cups graham cracker crumbs

½ cup almonds, ground

4 tablespoons sugar, divided

¼ cup vegan butter, melted

2 (8-ounce) containers vegan cream cheese

1 tablespoon lemon zest

1 tablespoon lemon juice

½ teaspoon salt

2 cups blueberries

Lemon, blueberries, and almonds seem healthy enough, but then add the cream cheese, graham crackers, sugar, and butter, and this goes squarely into the junk food category. No muss or fuss with these tangy-sweet bars.

« – »

1. Line a 9" × 9" baking dish with parchment paper, slightly overlapping edges to make it easier to remove bars from dish.

2. In a medium bowl, combine graham cracker crumbs, almonds, 2 tablespoons sugar, and butter until well combined. Press into prepared baking dish.

3. In a stand mixer or by hand, beat cream cheese, 2 tablespoons sugar, lemon zest, lemon juice, and salt. Pour over crust, spreading evenly. Top with blueberries.

4. Refrigerate at least 4 hours or overnight. Cut into bars.

NO-BAKE PEANUT BUTTER CUP BARS

Peanut butter plus chocolate, the no-bake version!

1. Line a 9" × 9" baking dish with parchment paper or waxed paper.

2. For crust: in a medium bowl, combine the crushed cookies, ¼ cup butter, and ¼ cup coconut oil. Press into prepared dish.

3. For the filling: in the same bowl, combine 1 cup peanut butter, powdered sugar, remaining ¼ cup coconut oil, and 2 tablespoons butter, stirring until smooth. Spoon onto crust, patting evenly to distribute. Refrigerate 30 minutes.

4. In a small saucepan over medium-low heat, melt the chocolate chips with remaining ½ cup peanut butter, stirring constantly. Pour over filling layer and refrigerate about 4 hours until set enough to cut into bars.

- 1½ cups finely crushed vegan peanut butter sandwich cookies (such as Nutter Butter Bites)
- ¼ cup plus 2 tablespoons vegan butter, melted, divided
- ½ cup coconut oil, melted, divided
- 1½ cups peanut butter, divided
- 1½ cups powdered sugar
- 1 (12-ounce) package vegan semisweet chocolate chips

NO-BAKE OATMEAL ALMOND BUTTER BARS

An oat drop cookie held together with a caramel almond butter mixture—perfect for when you forgot to bake something but committed to bringing dessert!

1. Line a cookie sheet with parchment paper. Lightly grease an 8" × 8" baking dish.

2. In a large saucepan over high heat, bring sugar, milk, and butter to a boil; stir constantly 2 minutes. Remove from heat. Stir in almond butter and vanilla.

3. Place oats in a large bowl and pour sugar mixture over oats. Mix well so that all the oats are coated.

4. Press into prepared baking dish. Set aside to firm, about 1 hour.

- 2 cups sugar
- ¼ cup nondairy milk
- ½ cup vegan butter
- ½ cup almond butter
- 1 teaspoon vanilla extract
- 3 cups uncooked quick oats

NO-BAKE BROWNIE BITES

» MAKES 1 DOZEN
BITES «

1 cup cashews

½ cup almonds

1 cup dates

2 tablespoons coconut oil

¼ cup cocoa powder

1 teaspoon vanilla extract

½ cup grated coconut, or ½ cup
   powdered sugar

Keep the oven off but break out the food processor to make these scrumptious bites. (Sometimes, simpler is junkier.)

« – »

1. In a food processor, process cashews and almonds until very finely chopped. Add dates, coconut oil, cocoa powder, and vanilla; process until very well blended.

2. Roll brownies in either coconut or powdered sugar.

PEANUT BUTTER BREAD *with* CREAM CHEESE FROSTING

» MAKES 10–12 SERVINGS «

2 cups flour

2 teaspoons baking powder

¼ teaspoon salt

⅓ cup sugar

¾ cup chunky peanut butter

1 cup nondairy milk

2 tablespoons ground flaxseeds

1 (8-ounce) container vegan cream cheese

1½ cups powdered sugar

Many people like to spread peanut butter on bread, but in this ingenious combo, you spread sweet cream cheese onto peanut butter bread. A nice twist, if you ask me.

1. Preheat oven to 350°F. Lightly grease a 9" × 5" loaf pan.

2. In a medium bowl, mix flour, baking powder, and salt.

3. In a small bowl, mix sugar, peanut butter, milk, and flaxseeds. Add to flour mixture and mix just until combined.

4. Pour into prepared loaf pan.

5. Bake 50 minutes.

6. In a stand mixer or by hand, beat cream cheese until light and fluffy. Add powdered sugar and mix until combined, about 2 minutes. Spread onto warm cake and allow to cool completely.

CHOCOLATE CHUNK BROWNIES

If you served these at a bake sale, you could easily charge double that of regular mix brownies. Box mix just seems lame after you taste one of these chunky, nutty beauties.

«– –»

1. Preheat oven to 350°F. Grease a 9" × 13" baking dish.

2. In a medium bowl, mix soy milk and apple cider vinegar. Set aside 5 minutes.

3. In a separate medium bowl, sift together flour, cocoa powder, baking soda, and salt.

4. Add sugar, oil, and vanilla to soy milk mixture; stir well. Add to dry ingredients and stir until smooth. Stir in chocolate and nuts. Pour into prepared baking dish.

5. Bake 30–35 minutes.

» MAKES ABOUT
A DOZEN BROWNIES «

¾ cup soy milk

1 tablespoon apple cider vinegar

2 cups flour

½ cup cocoa powder

1 teaspoon baking soda

1 teaspoon salt

1½ cups sugar

¾ cup oil

1 teaspoon vanilla extract

1 cup vegan semisweet chocolate chips

½ cup nuts (almonds or hazelnuts), roughly chopped

MOCHA CHEESECAKE BROWNIES

¾ cup soy milk

1 tablespoon apple cider
 vinegar

2 cups flour

½ cup cocoa powder

1 teaspoon baking soda

1 teaspoon salt

1½ cups sugar

¾ cup oil

1 teaspoon vanilla extract

1 (8-ounce) container vegan
 cream cheese

½ cup powdered sugar

3 tablespoons strong black
 coffee

Imagine taking your morning mocha, a rich, creamy cheesecake, and fudgy brownies and putting them in a blender—that's what you've got here. Of course, not in terms of consistency, but the flavors meld in a way that's truly sublime.

« – »

1. Preheat oven to 350°F. Grease a 9" × 13" baking dish.

2. In a medium bowl, mix soy milk and apple cider vinegar. Set aside 5 minutes.

3. In a separate medium bowl, sift together flour, cocoa powder, baking soda, and salt.

4. Add sugar, oil, and vanilla to soy milk mixture and stir well. Add to dry ingredients and stir until smooth. Pour into prepared baking dish.

5. In a medium bowl, stir together cream cheese, powdered sugar, and coffee until completely mixed. Drop by heaping tablespoonfuls onto brownie mix. Using a butter knife, swirl cream cheese mixture gently into brownie batter.

6. Bake 35–40 minutes.

CRISPY BROWNIE SQUARES

Favor crisp over chewy? If so, this is the junk food for you: a brownie masquerading as a flat cookie bar topped with crunchy almonds.

« – »

¼ cup coconut oil

3 tablespoons cocoa powder

½ cup sugar

1 tablespoon cornstarch

1 teaspoon vanilla extract

½ teaspoon salt

¼ cup flour

⅓ cup almonds, finely chopped

1. Preheat oven to 400°F. Line two 8" × 8" baking dishes with lightly greased parchment paper, slightly overlapping the rim to make it easier to remove brownies later.

2. In a medium saucepan over medium-low heat, melt coconut oil with cocoa powder, stirring constantly until smooth. Remove from heat.

3. Stir in sugar, cornstarch, vanilla, salt, and flour until well blended.

4. Spread half of batter into each baking dish and sprinkle with nuts.

5. Bake 12 minutes or until top is firm to the touch.

6. Cool 4 minutes and then cut brownies into small squares. Then cool completely in baking dish. Using parchment, lift brownies out of pans.

WHITE CHOCOLATE LEMON BROWNIES

» MAKES 8–10 BROWNIES «

8 tablespoons vegan butter

2 cups vegan white chocolate chips, divided

½ cup brown sugar

Zest of 3 medium lemons

2 tablespoons lemon juice

¼ cup silken tofu, blended smooth

1¼ cups flour

A white brownie! It's lemony with a smooth white-chocolate flavor and studded with more white chocolate chips. The addition of tofu makes it dense and moist.

« – »

1. Preheat oven to 325°F. Line a 9" × 9" baking dish with parchment paper.

2. In a large saucepan over medium-high heat, melt butter and 1 cup white chocolate chips, stirring constantly until smooth. Allow to cool until mixture is no longer hot, stirring occasionally. Add brown sugar, lemon zest, lemon juice, and tofu, stirring until well combined.

3. Stir in flour and remaining 1 cup white chocolate chips.

4. Pour batter into prepared baking dish.

5. Bake 40 minutes.

6. Allow to cool, then refrigerate overnight. Cut into bars.

Index

Note: Page numbers in **bold** indicate recipe category lists in Table of Contents.